PROFILING IN PRIMARY SCHOOLS

Profiling in Primary Schools

A Handbook for Teachers

Edited by
Ron Ritchie

With Contributions by
David Coulby, Linda Fursland, Stephen Ward,
Kay Wood, Sally Yates (Bath College of Higher Education)
and Keith Sadler (Adviser for Assessment, Avon)

CASSELL

Cassell
Villiers House   387 Park Avenue South
41/47 Strand   New York
London   NY 10016-8810
WC2N 5JE   USA

First published 1991

British Library Cataloguing-in-Publication Data
A catalogue record for this book is available from the British
Library.

ISBN   0-304-32450-7

Library of Congress Cataloging-in-Publication Data
Ritchie, Ron, 1952–
     Profiling in primary schools : a handbook for teachers / Ron
Ritchie
        p.   cm. -- (Cassell education series)
     ISBN 0-304-32450-7
     1. Personnel records in education.   I. Title   II. Series
     LB2845. 7.R58   1991
     372. 12--dc20
                                              91-20681
                                              CIP

Layout by Chris Pink at Bath College of Higher Education.
Printed and bound in Great Britain by Hollen Street Press Ltd, Slough

Contents

This book was produced in association with Avon Education Authority through the Bath Assessment Group based at Bath College of Higher Education.

General Aims of the Book

1.   To encourage the implementation of effective record-keeping as an aspect of a whole-school policy on assessment;

2.   To develop teachers' understanding of profiling as a process for recording children's curricular and personal achievements that reflects the school's aims in practice;

3.   To explore issues related to profiling and its implementation in primary schools;

4.   To introduce and explore a variety of strategies for profiling in terms of curriculum planning and organization.

Introduction

> *They say that no one truly sees his own face. This mercy of nature comes from the fact that reflections in a mirror show partial pictures which are flat; they cannot show an object in the round. To see an object in the round it must be observed as a whole in three dimensions. The skills of young children show reflections of their attainment, but they do not show attainment in the round. To see their attainment in the round we must observe it in their way of living.*

> Christian Schiller, *The Assessment of Attainment of Young Children*, Ministry of Education discussion paper (1946)

This material is designed to help you obtain and record a 'rounder picture' of children. All teachers keep some records of children's achievement and progress since, as the National Curriculum Council (NCC) stated in *An Introduction to the National Curriculum* (1989), 'record-keeping provides a mechanism through which teachers can focus on the needs and attainment of the individual child'. We hope that working through the tasks included in this book will encourage you to look at the nature and purposes of your own recording. You should then be able to modify and develop your existing approach in order to meet the school's aims and to meet the needs of the children, yourself as their teacher, their parents/carers and other outside agencies.

We regard assessment as the means by which teachers gain insight into learning. Consequently, teaching and assessment are inextricably linked in a way that means the process of assessment is an essential element of effective teaching. Recording, though important, is only one part of the assessment process and is not an end in itself, as Figure 1 indicates.

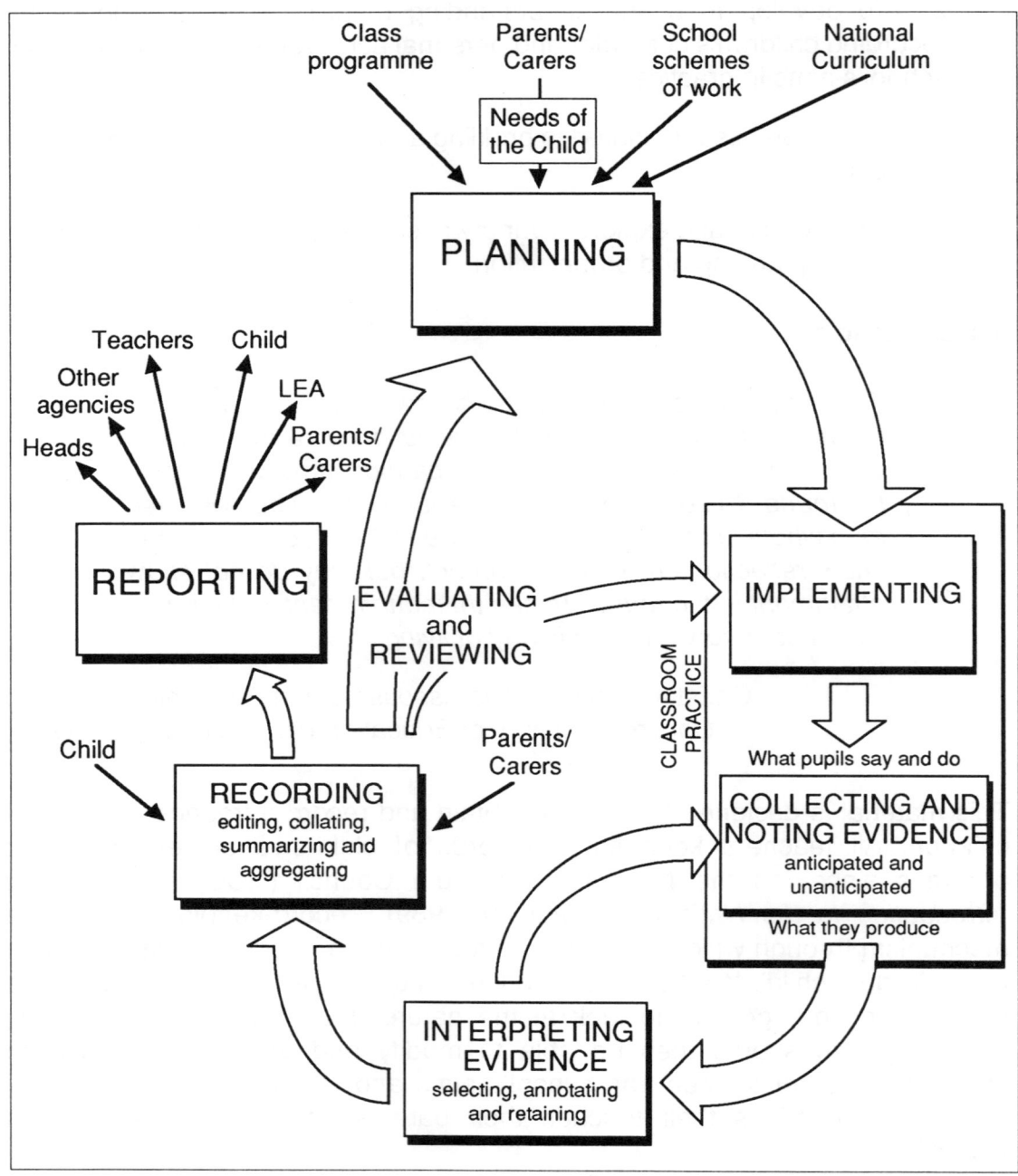

Figure 1: The Assessment Process

Record-keeping needs to be considered in the context of curriculum planning, assessment and reporting. Hence this book is intended to complement other materials produced by the School Examinations and Assessment Council (SEAC) and the National Curriculum Council (NCC).

The demands of the National Curriculum have led to a proliferation of tick sheets and summary cards of various sorts. Such methods of recording can have serious limitations and often simply provide a record showing that children have been offered particular experiences rather than providing any information about what they gained from them. Similarly, records of an individual's progress can be extremely restricted if they consist only of levels, marks and short summative comments. They can fail to provide useful information and may often be misleading. Working through this book should help you become more critical of certain recording strategies and enable you to design and implement recording methods that suit your own and your school's particular needs. It is impossible for teachers to record everything and there is a need to be selective about the evidence of learning collected. The judgements that have to be made in this selection are the key to effective record-keeping.

The following units should help you appreciate the value of records that include children's achievements within and outside school. The extent to which records should cover subject assessments, cross-curricular skills, personal and social skills, achievements and experiences will be explored. You will also be asked to consider the role of the individual child and their parents/carers in the process of record-keeping. All school record-keeping systems now have to meet the statutory requirements of the Education Reform Act and the materials invite you to examine the implications of this.

Profiling is a process that involves teachers, children and their parents/carers in assessing and recording the child's achievements across a range of curricular and extra-curricular areas, using a variety of assessment strategies. Teachers, children and their parents/carers work in partnership to enable a rounded picture of the child to be recorded. Profiling has many advantages over other processes of recording.

It can encourage curriculum unity rather than fragmentation and encompasses a formative process, which assists teaching, as well as a summative statement of achievements. A key strategy for profiling involves one-to-one dialogue between teacher and child. This may involve *reviewing,* which is usually a dialogue with a specific curriculum focus, or *conferencing*, in which the dialogue is more open-ended and the child is invited to take the initiative.

The tasks included in the following units address key questions such as:

What is profiling?

Why profile?

What should be profiled?

Who contributes to a profile?

How should we profile?

What problems are likely to occur?

How can profiling become effective throughout the school?

The extensive work already done in secondary schools on profiling and Records of Achievement is drawn upon in the materials to inform the development of profiling in primary schools. There are many examples of good record-keeping already evident in primary schools, but it is hoped that teachers will recognize within the readings provided aspects of secondary experience from which we can learn. In particular the national evaluations that have been carried out provide considerable evidence of aspects of profiling that are problematic and need to be carefully thought through. There are aspects of implementing profiling that do not require every school to re-invent the wheel. However, there are also key decisions that do need to be taken by every school and individual teacher about the particular needs of the children and context in which they work.

The answers to the problems of assessing and recording children's learning are not simple and will not be found within these pages. The answers lie within each individual teacher's classroom work and this book aims to help you search out your own solutions through classroom enquiry activities and reflective practice.

Using the Book

This package is not designed to be worked through from cover to cover. It is assumed that individual teachers and the staffs of schools will wish to adapt and use the materials to suit their individual and institutional needs.

The sections Section A includes readings and tasks that set the scene and provide an introduction to profiling from a variety of perspectives. Most of the tasks are suitable for staff discussions, although you are invited to begin to try out strategies in your classroom as a result of reflecting on your existing practice. These units refer to later units in Section B which provide more detailed and systematic treatment of issues concerned with the implementation of profiling. These can be used as and when work on the initial units indicates it would be valuable or appropriate.

The tasks Some tasks are designed for individual teachers; others are intended to be carried out by two teachers working collaboratively and others are to facilitate whole-staff discussions. However, most lend themselves to being adapted to meet particular needs. There is also material to support work with parents/carers, governors and other schools (from which children are received or to which they are sent).

Where to start Reading the overview and working through Section A should help identify priorities which can be tackled by using Section B units. A prioritizing activity, such as getting each member of staff to rank the Section B titles in the order of his or her own concerns, can help in this respect. Analysis of the lists should indicate appropriate starting points. Maximum benefit will be gained from the materials if their use is negotiated by the whole staff and a coherent approach is agreed. This will involve appropriate time set aside at staff meetings for activities and, if possible, time for teachers to work together in each other's classrooms.

Use of terms In this book, *assessment* is used to describe the process of gaining insight into an individual's learning; and *evaluation* is regarded as a process of deciding whether the teaching or learning intentions were appropriate and whether they were achieved. The terms *profiling* and *Records of Achievement (RoA)* are often used interchangeably. In the material we have used the term *profiling* to describe the process of compiling assessment information and *RoA* when referring to specific RoA initiatives and projects. A glossary is included at the end of the book.

The units Each unit is made up of one or more related activities. The following units are included in Section A (Adopting a Strategy for Profiling):

A1. Background to profiling

A2. National Curriculum requirements

A3. Reviewing children's progress

A4. Perspectives on profiling

A5. Elements of profiles

In Section B (Implementing and Evaluating Profiling) the key units are:

B1. Analysing and evaluating existing record-keeping

B2. Teachers' *pictures* of children

B3. Meeting legal requirements

B4. Self-assessment

B5. Liaising with others

B6. Recording evidence of learning

B7. Recording personal qualities

B8. Knowledge of children outside the classroom

Each unit has a Title and the headings Aims, Introduction, Method, Follow-up, Background information (where appropriate) and Bibliography. The follow-up section includes review activities and in some cases indicates a suitable focus for classroom enquiries that encourage implementation of a particular aspect of profiling within the ordinary classroom context. Figure 2 shows how the units are linked.

Figure 2: A map of the units

A: Adopting a strategy for profiling

A1: Background to profiling	A2: National Curriculum requirements	A3: Reviewing children's progress	A4: Perspectives on profiling		A5: Elements of profiles
			A4a: The child's perspective	A4b: The teacher's perspective	
B2a: **Teachers' *pictures* of children**	B3a: **Meeting legal requirements**	B4: **Self-assessment**	B5: **Liaising with others**	B6: **Recording evidence of learning**	B7a: **Recording personal qualities**
B2b: Using research findings to improve teachers' *pictures* of children	B3b: Access to children's records	B4a: Making criteria for success explicit to children	B5a: Evaluating contacts with parents/carers	B6a: Collecting, selecting and retaining evidence of learning	B7b: Methods to assess and record personal qualities
B2c: Improving children's self-image		B4b: Using children's self-assessment	B5b: Involving parents/carers in profiling	B6b: Using children's recording	B8a: **Knowledge of children outside the classroom**
B2d: Conferencing with children		B4c: Encouraging children's self-assessment as well as teacher assessment	B5c: Teachers' skills and conferences with parents/carers	B6c: Selecting children's work for the profile	B8b: Conferencing with children about life out of school
B1a: **Analysing and evaluating existing record-keeping**		B4d: Using self-assessment to enable children to identify progress	B5d: Liaising with other schools	B6d: Recording information about context	B8c: Carrying out a conference with the child on home background
B1b: Summative and formative approaches to record-keeping		B4e: Learning about classroom ethos from children	B5e: Liaising with governors		B8d: Profiles and home background – issues and problems
B1c: Evaluating strategies for record-keeping					

B: Implementing and evaluating profiling

Aims of Each Unit

A. Adopting a strategy for profiling

A1 Background to profiling

To consider the background to the development of profiling and the context out of which it has arisen;

To appreciate the potential of profiling for changing relationships within school.

A2 National Curriculum requirements

To evaluate the contribution of profiling in the context of legal requirements associated with assessing and recording achievement within the Education Reform Act (1988).

A3 Reviewing children's progress

To introduce and clarify the key profiling activity of reviewing children's progress and to distinguish it from conferencing;

To develop aims and strategies for reviewing children's progress.

A4 Perspectives on profiling

A4a To raise and consider from the child's perspective the issues of motivation, self-esteem, ownership and control;

To evaluate the contribution of profiling to the child's development.

A4b To raise and consider, from the teacher's perspective, issues of children's motivation and learning styles, resources and time, ownership and control;

To evaluate the contribution of profiling to professional development.

A5 Elements of profiles

To consider the possible formats for the profile and the appropriateness of these for the particular school context.

B. Implementing and evaluating profiling

B1 Analysing and evaluating existing record-keeping

B1a To analyse the school's existing record system in relation to summative and formative assessment.

B1b Summative and formative approaches to record-keeping

To clarify the distinction between *formative*, *summative* and *diagnostic* assessment;

To help teachers to see the limitations of summative assessment and the value in formative assessment for the planning process.

B1c Evaluating strategies for record-keeping

To explore which strategies successfully enable record-keeping to be a part of a realistic classroom routine.

B2 Teachers' *pictures* of children

B2a To examine in greater depth the pictures we have of individual children in the classroom.

B2b Using research findings to improve teachers' *pictures* of children

To reconsider the picture we have of individual children in the light of evidence from research sources and to consider the degree of subjectivity or objectivity employed in the pen portraits.

B2c Improving children's self-image

To investigate children's self-image in the classroom with a view to enhancing self-esteem.

B2d Conferencing with children

To explore child conferences as a means of helping us to understand more about the child and his/her feelings/attitudes towards school.

B3 Meeting legal requirements

B3a To ensure that the school's record-keeping procedures allow legal requirements to be met but are not confined or constrained by them;

B3b Access to children's records

To consider the legal requirements in terms of access to individual records.

B4 Self-assessment

B4a Making criteria for success explicit to children

To investigate how far making criteria for success explicit to children affects and enables their learning, and the assessment and recording of their learning.

B4b Using children's self-assessment

To use children's self-assessment as a tool in formative assessment.

B4c Encouraging children's self-assessment as well as teacher assessment

To plan a piece of work that involves both self-assessment and teacher assessment.

B4d Using self-assessment to enable children to identify progress

To utilize profiles to enable children to identify the progress they have made and to stimulate further success.

B4e Learning about classroom ethos from children

To use children's evaluations of classroom ethos and classroom life to aid the teaching and learning process.

B5 Liaising with others

B5a Evaluating contacts with parents/carers

To evaluate existing contacts between parents/carers and the school.

B5b Involving parents/carers in profiling

To explore the role of parent/carer conferences in profiling;

To provide guidance for meetings with parents/carers to discuss aspects of profiling;

To consider issues related to parents'/carers' conferences.

B5c Teachers' skills and conferences with parents/carers

To consider the skills teachers need to run successful parents'/carers' conferences.

B5d Liaising with other schools

To decide what liaison on record-keeping should be developed with other schools, including linked schools in other phases.

B5c Liaising with governors

To explore the role of governors in relation to profiling and school record-keeping policy.

B6 Recording evidence of learning

B6a Collecting, selecting and retaining evidence of learning

To provide experience of working collaboratively with a colleague to collect evidence of children's learning.

B6b Using children's recording

To evaluate which examples of children's outcomes provide the most useful evidence of learning;

To explore ways in which children can record their own achievements.

B6c Selecting children's work for the profile

To help teachers to discuss and decide on a school policy for selecting and storing children's work as evidence of learning.

B6d Recording information about context

To investigate what information about the context of a child's work needs recording.

B7 Recording personal qualities

B7a To consider the value of and concerns about the assessment and recording of personal qualities as part of a child's profile.

B7b Methods to assess and record personal qualities

To evaluate methods which could be used in the assessment and recording of personal qualities as part of a child's profile.

B8 Knowledge of children outside the classroom

B8a To help teachers to consider their awareness of children's interests, knowledge, achievements and relationships outside school and the relevance of this to profiling.

B8b Conferencing with children about life out of school

To introduce the idea of conferencing with children for the purposes of profiling and consider some of the techniques involved in talking with individual children.

B8c Carrying out a conference with the child on home background

To carry out a conference with the child about aspects of her /his home background.

B8d Profiles and home background – issues and problems

To consider the issues and problems involved in using information about children's home background in the profile.

National Curriculum:
Some Myths and Realities

Keith Sadler (Adviser for Assessment, Avon LEA)

1. The introduction of a National Curriculum 5–16

The final arrangements for National Curriculum Key Stage 1 are far removed from the proposals first published in July 1987, and many educationalists now believe that the arrangements are likely to have the desired effect of enhancing learning opportunities, and outcomes, for children, and thus meet the Government's stated central purposes of raising educational standards.

The introduction of an imposed National Curriculum originally led to a whole range of apprehensions being raised by primary teachers, not least of which was the fear of having to work to an apparently prescriptive curriculum that was concerned with content rather more than with process. This fear seemed to be realized when the first Department of Education and Science publication *The National Curriculum 5–16: a Consultation Document* was published in July 1987 (DES, 1987). Even its uncompromising typewritten form seemed to give the message of 'back to basics' and many primary teachers believed that issues such as control, discipline and efficiency would be promoted to the detriment of broader process issues.

The outlined proposals appeared to contrast with a style of learning that depended on children working collaboratively in a cross-curricular manner, and many teachers felt that their professionalism was under attack. Worst of all, a series of ten 'subjects' – and the rigorous testing of those subjects – was promoted as the driving force of the curriculum. Such suggestions seemed to be the antithesis of the principles of those educators whose beliefs rested on the promotion of a positive self-image, independence, self-discipline and the development of personal and cultural values which would enable children to gain an understanding of the knowledge presented. Such an educational vision depended on ensuring that children were offered an appropriate balance between content and process. The fear was that if the processes that provide the context for accessing the content of the curriculum were to be diminished, then the educational whole would be diminished.

The July 1987 document stated that there would be a series of 'Task Groups' set up to make proposals for the development of a National Curriculum. The first of these, the Task Group on Assessment and Testing (TGAT), set the parameters and provided the central thread through which all the subsequent curriculum working groups would operate. When published, the TGAT report (TGAT, 1988) was applauded by many teachers as an outstanding and reassuring contribution. There was some hope that such a forward-thinking document, produced in a very short time in an atmosphere of interventionist hostility, could well provide a framework which was rather less fearsome than many had imagined. TGAT proposed that teacher judgements should be the starting point for National Curriculum assessment, and that Standard Assessment Tasks should be applied at the end of a Key Stage to confirm teachers' judgements. This TGAT proposal was made at a time when many feared a rather less visionary document, based on external norm-referenced testing rather than internal formative and criteria-referenced assessment and, although there remained major concerns regarding the manageability of the proposals, these did appear to support teachers' professionalism.

2. The emerging National Curriculum

But still teachers had a whole series of questions to be answered. One deep concern stemmed from the belief that the TGAT report did not reflect an appropriate philosophy of learning. It is evident, for example, that children do not learn in an incremental manner, moving smoothly from one level of attainment to the next; yet TGAT proposed that the National Curriculum was to be described in such a manner through the use of ten levels of attainment. Furthermore, there was the obvious doubt that, however earnest and assiduous, the subject working groups would not get the levels in the right order. A second concern centred on the issue of the reporting of results, and the consequent dangers of narrowing the curriculum by teaching to the tests, particularly in the competitive environment of Local Management of Schools.

However, many of the fears of a fundamentalist, reductionist curriculum were laid to rest as the various subject working groups' reports began to emerge. In fact a new series of consistent realities became increasingly apparent. The terms of reference for the working groups demanded that any proposals made should be based on what amounts to a rigorous analysis of the over-arching aims of the curriculum area being considered. Hence, in Mathematics, the working group was told to outline 'the contribution of mathematics to the overall school curriculum' which should take account of 'best practice and the results of relevant research and curriculum developments' (DES, 1988, p. 91). This rigorous analysis of curriculum goals revealed the process of schooling to be not so much a means whereby our young are taught a series of firm and discrete subjects, but rather more as a subtle, complex and diffuse process which needs to bear in mind a multiplicity of purposes and ends.

In English, the terms of reference were sufficiently broad to enable the working group to build on a series of universal principles such as those outlined in the Bullock Report (DES, 1975). The group devised three separate profile components: Speaking and Listening, Reading and Writing, and took account of current research (DES, 1989a). Hence, the speaking and listening profile component built on the work of the National Oracy Project (at that time a School Curriculum Development Committee project), which has proved to be a highly effective means through which teachers' awareness and understanding of issues relating to speaking and listening have been greatly enhanced (National Oracy Project, 1989). The writing profile component developed from National Writing Project processes and materials. Even the most sceptical critics of the National Curriculum would find little to argue with the English document, which has been almost universally acclaimed as a forward-looking document that will do much to enhance the teaching of English. It demands a very broad based vision of English, and taken as an entirety, including the non-statutory guidance, it can be viewed as a sort of up-dated Bullock Report.

Similarly in Mathematics (DES, 1989b), we are left not so much with basic arithmetic, but with a process of mathematical development consistent with the sort of good practice which was espoused in the Cockcroft Report (DES, 1982). The document demands a broad and balanced mathematics diet, based not so much on pupils working through a published text, as on children developing understanding of mathematics by the use of investigations and problem-solving activities.

The Science document (DES, 1989c) is a similarly liberal document which places an equal emphasis upon process and knowledge. National Curriculum Technology (DES, 1990) confirms the processes of developing a technologically competent youngster . The document clearly emphasizes the necessary skills but it also is emphatic, through the definition of attainment targets, in the belief that the technological process is as critical to development as the skills and content demanded.

3. National Curriculum assessment arrangements

As well as the individual subject documents, the final assessment arrangements for Key Stage 1 have emerged as being very different from the simplistic summative tests that many feared. The TGAT principles have been adopted, and the teacher is placed at the centre of the process, with a limited role for external assessment. TGAT originally proposed the use of Standard Assessment Tasks (SATs) to provide an objective check on all the teacher assessments. However, no such instruments existed and these had to be created and trialled. The trial processes took three consortia of agencies £6 million and a 2 per cent pilot of year 2 children to prove that a summative assessment of pupils across all the Attainment Targets would not be manageable, would be disruptive, counter-productive and rather less than desirable. The final criteria for Standard Assessment Tasks require teachers to work on them for thirty hours over half a term (excluding English AT2). Furthermore, in stating that only seven Attainment Targets *have* to be assessed by SATs, and two others by 'constrained choice', the first TGAT principle of depending on the professionalism of teachers is being maintained.

Hence the National Curriculum Key Stage 1 as it now stands is very different in reality from the austere proposals of July 1987. Whilst many teachers are still fearful of its being debilitating to many children, others feel that it will offer a whole new range of entitlements for children.

4. National Curriculum and profiling in the primary school

Strategically, National Curriculum documentation and processes demand that the educational service addresses the two themes of progression and continuity, and many observers of schools, including HMI, have stated that these are two areas which schools need to consider because they are the two aspects of educational development which are central to the provision of a cohesive, effective and purposeful educational system. No scheme of work, teaching and learning style or development of policy is worthwhile if the issues of continuity and progression are not considered. If the National Curriculum can support teachers, schools and local authorities in devising strategies to meet the development needs of children in progression and continuity, then that in itself would begin to justify the introduction of a National Curriculum.

One way of ensuring curriculum continuity across a whole school, and indeed between phases of schools, is for teachers to work together to devise a profiling system. The development of a profiling system which records children's attainments and achievements, not just those of either the National Curriculum or the school, which will enable parents to be involved in the whole process, and which builds on an individual child's achievements, can be the most effective way of clarifying curriculum provision and thus providing continuity between classes and schools. A school's profiling system can act as the spine which draws all the learning strands together to meet the children's educational needs. If the development of a school profiling system supports the development of a whole-school assessment policy and, at the same time, draws parents into the process, promotes continuity of learning, and encourages children to be more responsible for their own learning, it is the one means through which all assessments, particularly formative teacher assessments, can be put into place.

References

DES (1975) *A Language for Life* (Bullock Report). London: HMSO.

DES (1982) *Mathematics Counts* (Cockcroft Report). London: HMSO.

DES (1987) *The National Curriculum 5–16: a Consultation Document.* London: HMSO.

DES (1988) *Mathematics for Ages 5 to 16: Proposals of the Secretary of State.* London: HMSO.

DES (1989a) *English in the National Curriculum.* London: HMSO.

DES (1989b) *Mathematics in the National Curriculum.* London: HMSO.

DES (1989c) *Science in the National Curriculum.* London: HMSO.

DES (1990) *Technology in the National Curriculum.* London: HMSO.

National Oracy Project (1989) *Talk.* York: NCC.

TGAT (1988) *A Report.* London: DES.

ADOPTING A STRATEGY FOR PROFILING

Unit A1

Background to Profiling

Aims

To consider the background to the development of profiling and the context in which it has arisen.

To appreciate the potential of profiling for changing relationships within the school.

Introduction

Teachers have always kept records of children's achievements but the nature of those records has changed in many schools as a result of initiatives to introduce profiling. Profiling originated in secondary and further education and it is therefore helpful to look at those initiatives in order to understand its development. In most cases the early projects were school- and LEA-based and the development of profiling has usually been from the bottom up. There is still evidence of a commitment to profiling at the grass roots, within schools and LEAs, particularly those where pilot projects were established and are developing. However, the history of the profiling movement and its introduction to schools has been a chequered one, partly as a result of shifting government policy on this issue (see Unit A2). Many secondary school teachers have been working with profiles and Records of Achievements for a number of years and have considerable experience of the advantages and disadvantages involved. Primary teachers have more recently recognized the advantages of profiling as a way of recording a *rounder* picture of children's achievements and providing continuity and progression within and between schools. It is seen by many primary teachers as a way of humanizing the National Curriculum recording and reporting requirements. Primary teachers are also finding, like their secondary colleagues, that profiling changes relationships within schools, between teachers and children and parents/carers and sometimes between the staff as well.

Method

Read the *Background information* accompanying this unit.

1   List the purposes of record-keeping in your class and school.

2   Discuss the extent to which the purposes of profiling/Records of Achievement identified by the DES are appropriate to your school and would enable you to meet your own purposes identified above. Are there others that you would add?

3   Identify key concepts and skills associated with profiles in primary schools

   a. for teachers;

   b. for children.

4   Engaging in the process of profiling changes the relationships between teacher and child, between teacher and parent/carer and even between teachers themselves and with the headteacher. Brainstorm, in a small group, the ways in which relationships between the following might be changed if profiling, including the possibility of an element of negotiation, were to be introduced in your school:

   a. between teacher and child;

   b. between teacher and parent/carer;

   c. between teachers in the same school;

   d. between teachers in the transfer context;

   e. between the headteacher and staff.

These issues are explored in later units (particularly B5 and B8).

Follow-up

1   Read through the philosophy underlying RoA, according to the PRAISE project, in the *Background information.*

2   Take each statement in turn and discuss the extent to which it is already part of your school's policy on, or approach to, assessment. If it is not, is it an aspect that you would wish to see developed and how might this be achieved?

3   What practical problems would you envisage developing in your school as a result of the adoption of such a philosophy?

4   What do you foresee as the advantages of the adoption of such a policy for your school?

If you wish to follow up the theme of the development of the teaching and learning process through the introduction of profiling you will find Units A3 and B4 helpful.

Background information

The origins of the profiling movement can be traced back to the Newsom Report (*Half our Future*) in 1963, which stated,

> *Boys and girls who stay at school until they are 16 may reasonably look for some record of achievement when they leave.*

However, it was not until the early 1970s that any developments along these lines were set in motion in secondary schools. Two of the early projects were 'Pupils in Profile' in Scotland (initiated by the Head Teachers' Association in 1972) and the 'Swindon Record of Personal Achievement' in Wiltshire. In the late 1970s and early 1980s the development of new courses in tertiary and secondary education, designed to meet the challenge of school-leaver unemployment, spearheaded a new approach to teaching, learning and assessment. The well-worn phrase uttered by secondary teachers to recalcitrant youngsters 'work hard and you'll get a job' no longer held true, if indeed it ever did. Instead there was an urgent need to find ways of motivating adolescents which were not necessarily dependent on the extrinsic rewards of the labour market and which, furthermore, accredited pupils positively for skills developed in addition to those assessed by external examinations.

This emerging curriculum in vocational education for pre- and post-16-year-olds was characterized by experience-based learning, the shifting of responsibility for learning from the teacher to the learner and a greater emphasis upon cross-curricular skills like problem-solving, co-operative learning and the promotion of increased personal and social awareness.These aims are very familiar to primary teachers! Assessment took on a new role for such courses, focusing upon the diagnosis of a wide range of learning needs and subsequent feedback informing the process of learning. This formative assessment then became the basis of discussion between teacher and student and a process of negotiation between these two was built into the model of assessment, enabling students to take charge of their own learning, analyse strengths and weaknesses and set targets for future achievements, academic, personal and social.

The documents which were produced as a result of this process of assessment were called *profiles* because they presented a portrait of the student's progress across a range of achievements, academic, personal and social. Profiles could be formative and/or summative, depending upon the stage in the students' career at which they were developed and the uses to which they were to be put. The process of assessing the student, using a variety of different methods of assessment, across a range of variables is termed profiling. Profiling usually includes opportunity for diagnostic feedback to the student which may be, although it is not always, open to negotiation with the tutor.

The development of profiling has been a grass-roots movement, beginning with the schools and then taken up by the DES. In 1983 the DES published a draft policy statement on Records of Achievement and the response to this indicated strong support for the principle of RoA. In 1984 the DES published a definitive policy statement setting forward the objective of mandatory RoAs for all school leavers by 1990. These records, which would only emphasize positive aspects of achievement, were to include three components: externally assessed achievements, internally assessed achievements and extra-curricular activities.

The policy statement identified four purposes for RoA:

i. **Recognition of achievement**. Records and recording systems should recognize, acknowledge, and give credit for what pupils have achieved and experienced, not just in terms of results in public examinations but in other ways as well. They should do justice to the pupils' own efforts and to the efforts of teachers and parents to give them a good education.

ii. **Motivation and personal development**. They should contribute to pupils' personal development and progress by improving their motivation, providing encouragement and increasing their awareness of strengths, weaknesses and opportunities.

iii. **Curriculum and organization**. The recording process should help schools to identify the all-round potential of their pupils and to consider how well their curriculum, teaching and organization enable pupils to develop the general, practical and social skills which are to be recorded.

iv. **A document of record**. Young people leaving school or college should take with them a short, summary document of record which is recognized and valued by employers and institutions of further and higher education. This should provide a more rounded picture of candidates for jobs or courses than can be provided by a list of examination results, thus helping potential users to decide how candidates could best be employed, or for which jobs, training schemes or courses they are likely to be suitable.

Pilot schemes were established to introduce RoAs in nine LEAs and from 1985 to 1988 a project was set up by the DES to evaluate the progress of these. This was called the PRAISE project (Pilot Records of Achievement in Schools Evaluation).

The PRAISE project report described the philosophy underlying RoA as following:

i. that assessment should be part of the educational process;

ii. that pupils should be equal partners with teachers in learning;

iii. that RoA should fulfil the requirement for positive, constructive, detailed records which would support learning in school and provide information for all potential users;

iv. that the processes of recording should develop the self-concept, self-confidence, self-esteem and motivation of pupils.

In recent years, several LEAs (such as Dorset, Somerset, Wigan and Manchester) have initiated profiling / Record of Achievement projects in their primary schools and have produced useful support material for teachers. This material can provide a useful starting point for discussions in schools and some is listed below.

Bibliography

Broadfoot, P. (1986) *Profiles and Records of Achievement.* London: Holt.

Broadfoot, P. (1987) *Profiles in Context.* London: DES FEU.

Munby, S. (1989) *Assessing and Recording Achievement.* London: Blackwell.

DES (1988) *Records of Achievement: A Report of the National Evaluation of Pilot Schemes.* London: HMSO.

Satterley, D. (1989) *Assessment in Schools.* London: Blackwell.

Somerset LEA (1990) *Records of Achievement in Somerset Primary Schools.* Yeovil: Somerset LEA.

Wigan LEA (1990) *Recording Achievements in Primary Schools.* Wigan: Wigan LEA.

Unit A2

National Curriculum Requirements

Aims

To evaluate the contribution of profiling in the context of the legal requirements associated with assessing and recording achievement within the Education Reform Act.

Introduction

The Education Reform Act of 1988 and its accompanying documents and legislation are notoriously equivocal about profiling and Records of Achievement. This is in spite of the commitment of funds for RoA pilot projects and evaluation by the DES during the time that Sir Keith Joseph was Secretary of State. This unit discusses the requirements of the Education Reform Act and considers the potential contribution to be made by profiles. It examines the legal requirements for schools in terms of recording and reporting children's achievements. The role of profiles in providing a means of record-keeping that will provide evidence to allow teachers to use their own assessments of children to challenge the results of Standard Assessment Tasks (SATs), if necessary, is then explored.

Method

Read the *Background information* accompanying this unit.

Working in small groups carry out the following activities:

1   Discuss the extent to which your existing record-keeping meets the statutory requirements of the Education Reform Act. What changes are necessary?

2   How much of the information on summary sheets used to record the statutory minimum information is useful to you as the child's teacher or the child's next teacher?

3   What other information is worth recording beyond the minimum required?

4   Is your existing record-keeping fit for the purpose of providing evidence of the quality of your assessments to enable you to challenge SAT results? Try and retain evidence of your assessments and how you made them for a small group of children over a period of several weeks.

Follow-up

1   With a colleague evaluate the evidence that is available. If you were an LEA moderator would you be satisfied with the evidence? Is it adequate to confirm that *your* judgements about a child are more accurate than those obtained through the use of SATs?

2   List the advantages and disadvantages of using profiles as a vehicle for transmitting the National Curriculum assessments to parents/carers and to other teachers, heads and the LEA.

Unit B6 explores the use of evidence of learning and how it can be summarized for reporting purposes.

Background information

The original consultation document from the DES on the National Curriculum, issued in 1987 (TGAT, 1988a), made no reference to profiles but, as is indicated below, they have subsequently featured in DES, NCC and SEAC material.

The Report of the Task Group on Assessment and Testing (TGAT), published in 1988, succeeded in allaying some of the fears of the education profession by its commitment to existing good practice in assessment including the formative and diagnostic functions of assessment and profiles. TGAT recommends the use of RoA as 'a vehicle for recording progress and achievement within the national assessment system'.

It was also proposed by TGAT that the national testing and moderation associated with the National Curriculum could provide a means of accrediting and validating some aspects of RoA. Thus TGAT proposed what appeared to be a positive role for RoA within the recording and reporting required by the National Curriculum and set out a means of developing RoA, since the dimension of accreditation and validation was already recognized as a weakness of many, if not all, existing schemes.

Comments made in response to the TGAT proposals revealed some dissatisfaction with the proposed role allocated to RoA under the National Curriculum system of assessment and testing. It was pointed out that the use of RoA merely as a vehicle for recording attainment target levels would jeopardize a fundamental purpose of RoA, namely that of bringing together teacher and pupil in dialogue and negotiation. TGAT's *Three Supplementary Reports*, published in March 1988 (TGAT, 1988b), attempted to defuse this problem by emphasizing the role of pupil negotiation in decision-making about which assessment tasks to take and when. Since TGAT is concerned with external reference and validity, any negotiation between pupil and teacher which might affect the actual test results is out of the question.

> *If negotiation could alter the result, this value would be lost,*
> *and public confidence in national assessment distributions*
> *would be put at risk.*

(TGAT, 1988b, para 17)

It is clear from this statement that for all its commitment to diagnostic assessment TGAT was not prepared to sacrifice the basis for comparisons which a national system of assessment and testing will bring. Thus there is a fundamental conflict between the philosophy of profiling, with its total commitment to formative assessment, and the system as envisaged by the Task Group on Assessment and Testing. This tension, between the formative and evaluative dimensions of assessment, is built into the whole of the system of assessment and testing under the Education Reform Act and it is difficult to see how these can be reconciled.

After July 1988, with the passing of the Education Reform Act and the establishment of SEAC (School Examinations and Assessment Council), the issue of RoA was looked at again. A letter from SEAC to the Secretary of State for Education and Science in July 1989 submits advice about RoA which had been requested by the DES earlier in the year. SEAC, on the basis of its consultations, strongly recommends to the Secretary of State that RoA 'have proved their value and should be required for use with pupils across the age range 5–16'.

> *It is therefore our firm view that regulations requiring all schools to maintain a record of achievement for each pupil between the ages of 5 and 16 should be promulgated under section 22 of the Education Reform Act.*
>
> (SEAC, letter to the Secretary of State for Education and Science, July 1989)

A bulletin issued by the DES on 16 August 1989 in the name of Mrs Angela Rumbold on 'Reporting Pupil Achievement under the National Curriculum' (DES, 1989) recommends to SEAC that reporting to parents on the National Curriculum subjects should take place at the end of each key stage, whilst reports to parents on general progress should take place on an annual basis. There is no mention here of RoA, in spite of SEAC's strong recommendations.

The statutory requirements (Statutory Instruments 1990, No.1381) for reporting children's achievements were laid before Parliament in July 1990 (DES, 1990a). They require headteachers to ensure written information is available for parents in the final year of each key stage. This must include the level of achievement in each foundation subject and in each profile component (PC). There must also be a statement explaining that the levels have been assessed in accordance with the statutory requirements and listing any instances where a child has been exempted from an attainment target (AT). Heads are also required to provide parents, when requested, with relevant data about their child's achievements within fifteen days. This means information about levels of achievement in each AT in foundation subjects. In other words, the record-keeping system of a school must ensure these levels are recorded. There is no statutory requirement for any narrative comment to accompany these levels, although as discussed below there may be sound reasons for schools to ensure there is more information available than just AT levels. For years other than the final year in a key stage the written information should give 'brief particulars of his achievements' in foundation subjects and 'any other subject or activity which form part of the school curriculum'. It could be argued that this aspect of reporting is only possible through the use of a profile. The information has to be sent to parents/carers not later than the end of July in each year.

The notes accompanying these regulations were titled 'Records of Achievement'– Circular No 8/90 (DES, 1990b). In them the Secretary of State notes that many schools and LEAs now operate RoA schemes. He commends the good practice that is now developing and stresses that the regulations set down a common, minimum foundation for reporting on pupils' progress. The notes state that the method of recording is best left to local discretion, although there is recognition that a common format for the core requirements (AT levels) is desirable and will be given further consideration by the DES. The purposes of RoA originally formulated by the DES in 1984 (see Unit A1) are restated in the notes and government support for them reaffirmed (although still not supported with the necessary funding or national statutory framework). The National Curriculum 'and RoA are integrally linked' and the underlying principles of both involve 'recognising positive achievements in all pupils' according to the DES. Indeed we are told the Secretary of State sees 'RoA as the means by which achievements across the NC and beyond can be most effectively reported to a range of audiences'. The notes include an annex which outlines the nature of summative documents which it states should 'be the property of the school leaver'.

Another important DES document that reached schools in July 1990 was the National Curriculum Assessment Arrangements. The significance of this in terms of profiling lies in what it says about the relationship between teacher assessments (TA) and SATs. On page 3 of the Statutory Orders can be found the following, 'the level of attainment determined by the teacher assessment shall, if the local education authority... determine that it represents the more accurate assessment of the pupil's achievements, be the level for the purposes of article 7 (Determination of attainment)'. This provides the opportunity for teachers to challenge SATs if the record-keeping system they use is fit for this purpose. LEAs will need to be offered evidence of the quality of judgements that an individual teacher is making. Profiling can offer such a system. The framework for recording achievements outlined in Unit A5 and developed throughout this material should provide an approach to recording children's achievements which can validate the teacher's capability as an assessor and provide the LEA with the necessary evidence to support that teacher in challenging SAT results. It should also provide a more satisfactory framework for discussing children's achievements with their parents than a list of numbers indicating levels in ATs.

Bibliography

TGAT (1988a) *A Report.* London: DES.

TGAT (1988b) *Three Supplementary Reports.* London: DES.

DES (1989) *Reporting Pupil Achievement under the National Curriculum.* London: HMSO.

DES (1990a) *The Education (Individual Pupils' Achievements) (Information) Regulations 1990: No 1381.* London: HMSO.

DES (1990b) *Records of Achievement: Circular No 8/90.* London: HMSO.

DES (1990c) *National Curriculum Assessment Arrangements.* London: HMSO.

Unit A3

Reviewing Children's Progress

Aims

To introduce and clarify the key profiling activity of reviewing children's progress and to distinguish it from conferencing.

To develop aims and strategies for reviewing children's progress.

Introduction

Essentially, profiling as a process is concerned with the dialogue between children and teachers. As we have seen in Unit A1, profiling has the potential to alter the nature of this dialogue and to change relationships within the school. In order to carry out profiling effectively teachers may have to develop new skills. These skills are concerned with interacting with children on an individual basis. In such interaction the emphasis moves away from the whole-class management and control issues with which teachers are mostly concerned to the establishment of individual relationships, in which children are enabled to talk freely and confidently about themselves and their achievements. There are two aspects to this dialogue between the child and the teacher. The first is referred to in this material as *reviewing* and is regarded as a dialogue focused upon the learning context and usually upon particular aspects of the child's learning. The rest of the work for this unit is concerned with developing the skill of reviewing. The second aspect is called *conferencing* with children. This is an open-ended approach to the dialogue in which the teacher's aim is to encourage the children to take the initiative in the interaction and to talk about what motivates and interests them. You will be able to follow up the notion of conferencing in Unit B8.

Method

1   **Reviewing your own work** With a colleague review your own achievement in a particular aspect of your work, following the sequence of phases (recalling, analysing, evaluating, synthesizing/target-setting) set out in the *Background information* of this unit. When both of you have carried this out discuss what you have done using the following questions as guidelines.

a.   How accurate do you consider your memories/perceptions to be of the particular learning experience under discussion? How difficult did you find it to recall this?

b.   Were you able to come to any understanding about particular patterns underpinning your learning achievements and difficulties? How hard did you find this? Were you helped by working with a colleague?

c.   Have you achieved a good balance in your evaluation between identifying strengths and weaknesses?

d.   Is your target-setting relevant to the learning task under discussion and realistic in the light of other pressures?

e.   Has working through this sequence of phases changed your thinking about any of the following:

i.   your interest in the learning task under discussion?

ii.   your commitment to your own development within this particular area or in general?

iii. your trust and confidence in the judgement of the colleague with whom you were working?

iv.   your trust and confidence in your own judgement?

v.   any other aspect?

2 **Reviewing with children** Consider the advantages and disadvantages of reviewing with children. What difficulties might arise and how could they be overcome?

3 **Teachers' skills needed for reviewing** Identify skills needed to carry out a successful review with a child. Compare your list with those identified in the *Background information*. Which of these skills do you feel you have and which need development? What are the implications for your classroom management?

4 **Portfolios and self-assessment** Discuss the relevance of portfolios of children's work and children's self-assessment to your particular situation. What examples of children's work are already retained in your class? Plan how you will use appropriate units to explore these areas further (Units B4 and B6 are particularly relevant).

Follow-up

1 Working with your colleague, plan a review to be carried out in the classroom with an individual child, group or with the whole class, following the four phases: recalling, analysing, evaluating, synthesizing/target-setting. Use the same curriculum focus as your colleague. Evaluate the effectiveness of this in terms of the above criteria. Try reviewing in other curriculum areas. Is reviewing valuable in all areas of the curriculum, or have you found it more useful in some areas than others?

If you would like to carry this work on reviewing further you should look at Unit B4c. After you have implemented this in your classroom, discuss with your colleague how the information you gained through this process could be appropriately recorded.

2 Has your classroom management changed in any way? Consider other strategies you can use to free yourself to work with individual children. Evaluate the potential of each in your own situation.

3   What strategies will help you develop your skills in this area further? Consider using a tape-recorder or asking a colleague to observe you reviewing with a child.

Background information

> *Reviewing can be defined as a process which involves an individual or a group reflecting upon an experience or experiences in the past, seeking to remember and to understand what took place and attempting to gain a clearer idea of what has been learned or achieved.*

(Munby, 1989)

The process of reviewing can involve four phases (Greenaway and Crowther, 1983, quoted in Munby, 1989):

i.   In the knowledge phase the child, aided by the teacher if necessary, recalls an event or series of events from the past. It is important that this can be done with a reasonable degree of accuracy or at least that the child can remember his/her own perceptions of the event(s) accurately. In view of this it is necessary that the reviewing should follow fairly shortly after the learning episode.

ii.   In the analysis / understanding phase the child, with the teacher's help, seeks to find a pattern in the learning achievements or difficulties in order to understand better what underlies them.

iii. In the evaluation phase judgements are made by both child and teacher concerning strengths and weaknesses manifested in the learning under review.

iv.   In the synthesis phase teacher and child decide together how the learning under discussion fits into an overall context, and plan the next and future steps. This last phase is more concerned with the target-setting, which would more naturally follow upon the process of reviewing than be an integral part of this.

Munby (1989) suggests that there is a continuous sequence of events involving planning, experiencing the learning activity, reviewing and target-setting leading on to further planning. The same model is enshrined in the 'plan, do, review' process of negotiated learning approaches adopted by some teachers.

Classroom strategies which facilitate the reviewing process

Profiling, portfolios of work and self-assessment are all ways in which this process of reviewing can be encouraged in the classroom. However, fundamental to the success of reviewing is the need for a system of classroom management which frees the teacher to work with individual children. This is often achieved through the establishment of a classroom ethos in which children respect the right of other children to individual attention. Some teachers formalize this with strategies like 'bubble time', which children recognize to be a time when the teacher and the child she is working with are not to be disturbed. It is suggested that these issues of classroom management are addressed before other aspects of this unit can be developed.

The process of profiling has been described in Unit A1. It involves determining the criteria by which children are to be assessed, across a range of variables, academic, personal and social. The teacher then assesses the child or the child assesses herself against these criteria. In the latter case opportunity is also provided for assessment by the teacher. Profiling encourages dialogue and negotiation between the teacher and child which, although time-consuming, can be very beneficial in terms of enabling all the phases of reviewing to take place. If you wish to follow up the use of explicit criteria and their effect on enabling learning you should look at Unit B4a. A key consideration is how information gathered during profiling should be selected, annotated, collated, summarized and retained in a profile. The decisions teachers make about this are fundamental to effective record-keeping and are explored in Unit A5.

In many schools the profile is compiled by the child under the teacher's guidance and is the property of the child throughout his/her school career and at transfer to the next stage. Compiling and contributing to the profile gives children the opportunity to engage in reviewing, particularly when looking back at past work and making decisions about what should be included in the profile.

In addition, many profiling schemes specifically include opportunities for children to review progress at particular times, sometimes with the involvement of parents/carers.

Children's portfolios or collections of work often form an important part of the profile, although sometimes portfolios are maintained independently. You are asked to consider the value and purposes of collecting such a portfolio in Unit B6c. In order to enable the portfolio to be used as the basis of discussions during reviews it is helpful if each entry in the portfolio is carefully annotated by the teacher, noting basic information such as the date, the nature of the task and the assessment criteria which it demonstrates, who selected the work and what should be the future targets for the child (see Unit B6d). A formal review can be carried out on a regular basis between the teacher in a one-to-one context with the child or with the parents/carers on occasions (see Unit B5a). The future targets to be achieved by the child are agreed with the teacher, written down and often signed by both.

Self-assessment can encourage children to be aware of themselves in relation to their work from a very early age, either as a part of the procedures described above, or as an independent tool enabling children and the teacher to monitor progress. You will be able to follow up the notion of children's self-assessment as a tool for formative assessment in Unit B4.

As well as classroom management skills, numerous other skills are needed by a teacher when engaging in one-to-one discussions. The following list indicates some of them:

>   active listening;
>   allowing for the child's agenda as well as the teacher's;
>   responsive and open-ended questioning;
>   pacing and allowing pauses in the dialogue;
>   relaxing the child by smiling, body language and seating arrangement;
>   avoiding superficiality and being patronizing.

Bibliography

Munby, S. (1989) *Assessing and Recording Achievement*. London: Blackwell.

Unit A4

Perspectives on Profiling

Introduction

In order to look at issues related to the introduction of profiling in primary schools this unit again draws on the experiences of secondary colleagues who have explored the implications of profiling from the child's and teacher's perspective.

An objective picture of the effects of profiles on participating schools has emerged from a national evaluation project entitled 'Pilot Records of Achievement in Schools Evaluation' (PRAISE). This project evaluated the development of profiles in the nine pilot LEAs, from 1985 to 1988. A report of the work of this project was produced along with five volumes of case studies. The former is entitled *Records of Achievement: Report of the National Evaluation of Pilot Schemes* (1988) and is available from HMSO.

Both report and case studies focus upon pupil and teacher perspectives in the secondary sector and provide valuable insights into the effect of the introduction of profiling. This section draws upon this research and encourages you to apply it to your own school situation. Please bear with the emphasis upon the secondary sector as this is the only extensive research which has yet been done and many of its findings are appropriate for the primary teacher.

The Child's Perspective

Aims

To raise and consider from the child's perspective the issues of motivation and self-esteem, ownership and control.

To evaluate the contribution of profiles to the child's development.

Introduction

What do children get out of profiles? What are some of the disadvantages for children as participants in such approaches? Many claims have been made for profiling, such as improved motivation, self-esteem and employment prospects. What foundation is there for such claims in terms of research evidence? Are any groups of children undermined by the profiling process, for example, on the basis of gender, race, class or special educational needs? The research evidence to answer these questions is limited to the secondary context and stems from PRAISE. The *Background information* for this unit looks at the findings of PRAISE in relation to the experience of participating pupils and seeks to answer questions concerned with motivation, ownership and control.

Method

1   Read the *Background information* accompanying this unit which discusses the findings about secondary pupils' experiences. Identify the issues that might apply in your school.

2   *Reviewing can take place at any age – it is just a question of finding the right strategies and language.*

Discuss the above statement and your existing or proposed reviewing strategies (Unit A3 provides more support in this area and would be worth consideration at this point). Discuss appropriate language for the age groups covered by your school. Trial and modify such plans. To what extent has your approach improved the children's motivation?

3   How important is privacy and confidentiality to the children with whom you work? Discuss the extent to which this aspect needs to be built into the whole-school approach and how it can be translated into practice in the classroom.

Follow-up

It has been suggested that to contribute to profiling children should:

    a.   discuss experiences with teachers and parents/carers;

    b.   relate new experiences to existing ideas and past experiences;

    c.   develop skills of negotiation;

    d.   take account of how others see them.

Which of these can most children already do?
What strategies will enable more children to demonstrate these features?

You may wish to try out some of these strategies at this point and evaluate the extent to which they are successful.

You can pursue the topic of enhancing children's self-esteem in the classroom by looking at Unit B2a.

Background information

(Evidence from the PRAISE *Report*)

Pupil motivation and self-esteem   The PRAISE *Report* indicates that there is evidence to suggest that many pupils have found the opportunity to talk on a one-to-one basis with teachers both helpful and motivating. There is also evidence to suggest that pupils in the case-study schools have grown in self-awareness and the ability to reflect upon academic progress and personal development, although it is difficult to disentangle the effects of profiles from those of other initiatives such as TVEI and GCSE.

At one of the case-study schools the following types of comment were made by fifth-year pupils after receiving their summative documents:

> *Preparing the RoA made you look at yourself.*

> *It helped me get to know myself.*

> *To be more confident in interviews, etc.*

> *It enabled me to learn to write about myself.*

> *I can write things in a better way.*

Younger pupils felt that reflecting on personal and academic achievements might help them to improve but were not prepared to admit to any direct changes as a result of engaging in profiles.

The evaluation of pupil motivation also provided evidence about individual differences.

a.   Girls showed themselves more able to reflect on their progress and to cope with the writing involved, whereas boys revealed a more developed sense of their external audience. Girls proved better at the formative aspects of profiles such as reflection on likes and dislikes; boys were better at the summative aspects, including recording of factual information like membership of teams.

b.   For pupils whose first language is not English preparing the profiles in their community language was a positive experience, although there is some concern as to whether this will be acceptable to employers and other 'end users'. Such pupils also benefited from the opportunity to engage in reviewing in a pair with another pupil who was also bilingual.

c.   Higher-attaining pupils were sometimes unconvinced of the value of profiles but carried them out conscientiously, whilst the lower-attaining pupils were hampered by the lack of literacy skills. However, many teachers had found alternative means of recording progress through pictures and tapes.

d.   Pupils' attempts at self-assessment were beset with problems: some were superficial in their self-assessments, others gave themselves particularly low ratings, others persisted in maintaining a norm-referenced approach by comparing themselves with others. Teacher expectations strongly influenced pupil perceptions of their progress, particularly when pupils requested help from the teacher in completing a review. Further work on helping children with self-assessment is to be found in Unit B4.

e.   Age differences proved to be an important variable in determining pupil motivation. Some of the younger boys were more likely to find the procedure 'boring' than the girls; the younger girls were more likely to be keen and enthusiastic. Among older pupils boys were sometimes more likely to be inhibited in writing about themselves and hence any personal statements written were shorter.

Ownership and Control   There is evidence to suggest that control of profiles in terms of ownership by pupils leads to a greater commitment on the part of the pupils. This ownership includes the recognition by teachers of pupils' rights and responsibilities, including the right to choose the contents of the profiles, the right to reject teacher comments perceived to be inaccurate and the right to privacy and confidentiality.

One scheme commented upon in the PRAISE *Case Studies* (DES, 1989) involved pupils in the use of a personal journal entitled a 'Think Book'. The purpose of this was to give them the opportunity to reflect upon personal and learning experiences and to provide a written medium of communication with the tutor, who read and commented upon the journals regularly. The issue about confidentiality regarding Think Books was discussed at length, both with pupils and in tutor meetings. Eventually this was resolved by classifying Think Books as 'private between pupil and tutor', meaning that pupils were discouraged from showing the record to friends and indeed no pupil was allowed to read another's Think Book without permission. Pupils could mark a particular passage in the Think Book as private and this wish would be respected by the tutor. Pupils could also request the tutor not to comment about a particular passage. In another school, where personal folders were stored in the staff room, some of the pupils obviously felt inhibited from writing anything private in the folder, as this quotation shows, 'No it's not worth risking (writing anything secret), anybody could just walk in and get it'.

Overall, the benefits of profiles for pupils were summed up by the PRAISE *Report* (DES, 1988) in the following quotation:

> *Some of the pupils we studied felt the provision of clearer objectives, personal targets and more supportive relationships with teachers had enabled them to make more progress than would otherwise have been the case. Pupils' personal recording and reviews have also helped teachers to become more aware in many cases of pupils' hitherto unknown personal achievements and this has enabled them to help pupils build on their strengths.*

Nevertheless, work that has been carried out on pupil differences in respect of profiles, some of which is cited above, suggests that these differences influence the extent to which pupils are able to benefit from profiles, just as they influence pupils' educational careers as a whole. The PRAISE *Report* indicates that more work needs to be done in this area of pupil differences if we are to be 'confident that the positive effects of profiles, which are already being documented, apply to more than a minority of pupils'.

You may find Unit B4a helpful if you wish to take this further.

Bibliography

DES (1984) *Records of Achievement.* London: HMSO.

DES (1988) *Report of the National Evaluation of Pilot Schemes.* London: HMSO.

DES (1989) *Pilot Records of Achievement in Schools Evaluation: Case Studies of Schools 1985–88 .Volume 1 (PRAISE)*. Bristol: University of Bristol.

The Teacher's Perspective

Aims

To raise and consider, from the teachers' perspective, issues of children's motivation and learning styles, resources and time, ownership and control.

To evaluate the contribution of profiles to professional development.

Introduction

From the teacher's perspective, profiling, like any other educational innovation, represents a trade-off between the availability of appropriate expertise, resources and time to accomplish the innovation and the benefits likely to accrue from it in terms of the development of children's learning and the professional development of teachers.

The research carried out by the PRAISE team, mentioned in Unit A4a, indicates that the potential benefits to accrue to pupils from profiles are considerable, although the extent to which these benefits are realized depends upon the ways in which profiling is carried out.

Method

Managing profiling   Read the *Background information* accompanying this unit, which places a strong emphasis upon getting the management of profiling right, both at the level of the whole-school approach and in terms of teaching strategies in the classroom.

1   Analyse your current strategies for assessment within the school in terms of the extent to which they give children responsibility for their own learning and involve them in reviewing and assessment.

2   Discuss strategies for involving the child and parents/carers more fully in assessment procedures and for encouraging them all to take responsibility for the child's learning (see Units B4, B5 and B8).

3   To what extent are issues about ownership relevant in the primary phase?

4   Would a summative document motivate children at Key Stages 1 and 2?

Follow-up

List all the practical difficulties of introducing profiles to your school. If you already operate such a system discuss the difficulties you are already experiencing. Discuss ways of overcoming these by establishing priorities. It may be helpful if at this point you actually show in rank order what you think the priorities of the school are currently in terms of resources, time, accommodation, etc. What needs to go or to be moved further down the list of priorities if profiles are to be successful? What savings can be made if profiles are introduced successfully, for example, by using formative statements as reports?

To what extent could a co-ordinator for profiling in school help to overcome the difficulties you have identified?

Discuss the role of a profiling co-ordinator in a primary school.

This would be a good point at which to discuss the use of Section B units, or to return to these discussions after you have looked at Unit A5.

Background information

Children's motivation and learning styles

Children are motivated in two ways, firstly by the procedures associated with profiling, which should encourage them to take some responsibility for their own learning, and secondly by the end product: the summative document which is owned by them and moves with them through their education and into employment.

There is evidence from the PRAISE *Report* that both of these factors influence secondary pupils' motivation:

> *Pupils' motivation is significantly improved to the extent that they are given responsibility for their learning and are involved in reviewing and assessment. Essex reported improved self esteem and higher expectations by both teachers and pupils.*

Both the developments in pupils' motivation referred to above are attributed to new approaches to teaching and learning on the part of the teachers where profiles are part of a whole-school policy about children becoming more autonomous in their learning styles. If you wish to follow this up by considering further the effects of profiles on motivation and self-image you will find Unit B2c very useful. Unit B4e draws attention to the interaction between styles of teaching and learning and the use of profiling techniques.

Only limited research has been carried out on the summative document. Although there is little evidence concerning the value of this to 'end-users' such as parents/carers, teachers in transfer schools and employers, there is evidence that secondary pupils themselves value the end product. Because of this many secondary schools have moved away from the sustained personal reflection required by log books, open-ended personal records and diaries towards the production of interim summative statements. Many fifth formers felt that this was something useful to show to an employer and others felt that learning about oneself in preparation for interview was helpful.

Teacher perspectives on resources and time

Resources are a major concern for the teacher and much of the publicity in the media about profiling has drawn attention to the need for extra time and space required, particularly for the reviewing between teacher and pupil(s). Time also needs to be set aside for the school's profiling co-ordinator, for the ancillary staff to prepare summative documents and for staff development. In addition, there are other resource implications arising from profiles including materials and equipment, computers, storage facilities and stationery.

It is clear from the PRAISE *Report* that the successful implementation of profiling does depend on additional resources being made available or upon the prioritization of resources from a budget which is under pressure from other sources, not least the assessment required by the Education Reform Act.

On the other hand, PRAISE shows that where teachers had integrated the procedures for profiles into their classroom management strategies, the time issue had become less of a problem, as teachers 'managed to make profiles a positive support to their teaching through providing for a more varied approach to pedagogy rather than regarding them simply as a time-consuming chore'.

Ownership and control

Profiles involve at least two different kinds of ownership; the first is that of the children to whom the contents belong at each stage of the process; the second is that of the school/LEA, where the issue is concerned with ownership of the processes and procedures which bring the profiles into being. In both these cases ownership is important as a means of deepening commitment to the task.

In the case of the child's ownership of the summative document, however, this does have to be reconciled with the need for this document to be appropriate for the needs of 'end-users', including parents/carers, teachers and employers. The National Curriculum also raises issues about the reality of the child's ownership of results of assessment over which they have no control.

The extent to which teachers hand over control of profiling procedures to children, as opposed to paying lip service to it, is also dependent upon the kind of system involved. The more open-ended the scheme for reviewing children's achievement, the more opportunity there is for children to reflect upon achievements and needs. Unit B4d also draws attention to this.

It is clearly important for the success of profiles that children and teachers feel a sense of ownership of the contents and processes in order to sustain the commitment which the implementation of profiling requires.

The PRAISE *Report* also draws attention to the need for a 'whole school' approach to profiles:

> profiles must be integrated into curriculum planning along with assessment, recording and reporting, as well as the pastoral system. This requires long term planning and structured strategies ... including ... the commitment and understanding of the senior management team.

Bibliography

DES (1984) *Records of Achievement.* London: HMSO.

DES (1988) *Records of Achievement: Report of the National Evaluation of Pilot Schemes.* London: HMSO.

DES (1989) *Pilot Records of Achievement in Schools Evaluation: Case Studies of Schools 1985–88. Volume 1.* Bristol: University of Bristol.

Unit A5

Elements of Profiles

Aims

To discuss the possible formats for profiles and to consider the appropriateness of these for the particular school context.

Introduction

There are two dimensions to any profile; the first is the child and the second is the curriculum. To a large extent the first dimension includes the second, particularly for younger children, but it is still helpful to draw the distinction between the two for the purposes of an in-depth scrutiny such as you are undertaking in this unit. A comprehensive profile would probably need to look at three aspects of the child: achievement, experiences and qualities. These are considered in the *Background information*. With regard to the curriculum a comprehensive profile would probably need to include subject-specific achievement and cross-curricular achievement. Also discussed in the *Background information* are possible formats for presenting profiles.

Method

Read the *Background information*.

1   The DES policy statement (DES, 1984) suggests that profiling systems should aim for comprehensive coverage. How desirable and/or possible do you feel this to be? Should profiles cover curriculum and extra-curricular achievements?

2   Is it valid to distinguish between the three aspects of the child as in achievements, experience and qualities? Is it possible to maintain these distinctions when keeping records about children? Can you suggest other recording categories for the child?

3   What will the curricular aspects of a profile need to contain? How might cross-curricular skills, processes and concepts be recorded?

4   Discuss elements for a profile suited to your school needs. Agree a series of targets for trialling various aspects and a date for reviewing progress.

5   Consider the following practical issues:

Format (ring binder, folder?)

Space for storage (classroom, office?)

Specified items for inclusion (DES report forms, curriculum summary sheets?)

Optional items for inclusion (child-selected work?)

Confidential elements

Child's access

Parent's/carer's access

Access of others (HMI, governors, visitors)

Final ownership

When does the school release the profile and to whom?

These issues are discussed further in Unit B6c.

6   Plan a strategy for establishing a whole-school approach to recording evidence of children's learning. It may be appropriate for the whole staff to try Unit B6a and use this as a basis for further discussion about the nature of the decisions involved. The emphasis could be on a curriculum area already identified in the Institutional Development Plan.

Follow-up

Review progress made after an agreed period. Collect examples of profiles from other schools and compare them with yours. Are there elements that you could adapt to improve your own models?

Background information

What information does a comprehensive profile on the child need to contain?

The introduction suggested that a comprehensive profile would need to look at three aspects of the child: achievement, experiences and qualities. These are now considered in turn.

a. Personal achievements, including interests and hobbies, and achievements in terms of awards. The latter may be carried out within the school or in school extra-curricular activities, in which case they can readily be authenticated by a member of the school staff, or out of school at home or at clubs unconnected with the school. This raises questions concerning authentication or proof of the validity of the child's claims. You may wish to take this further by studying Unit B8.

b. Experiences, looked at in terms of the child's participation, both within and outside the school. Again there is the issue of authentication of experiences outside the school context. Unit B8 is very useful for a further consideration of this issue.

c. Personal qualities such as perseverance, loyalty, etc. (Note the difference between aspects of personality, for example, humour and less stable characteristics such as punctuality.) These may be recorded directly, as qualities, with or without supporting evidence, or inferred from recorded evidence of experiences or achievements. Clearly the issue of recording personal qualities raises a number of questions concerning bias and subjectivity on the part of the assessor. You will find Units B2 and B7 take the issue of bias and subjectivity in teacher judgements about personal qualities much further.

What information does a comprehensive profile on the child's curricular achievements need to contain?

a.   First, there are subject-specific achievements, including National Curriculum core and foundation subjects and probably any other subjects not included in the National Curriculum like health education. The statutory requirements, outlined in Unit A2, mean it is necessary to allocate a considerable amount of space to the recording of subject-specific achievement, since there are forty attainment targets for the three core subjects alone.

b.   Second, there are cross-curricular achievements, including communication skills and information-processing skills. These do not currently feature in the National Curriculum assessment requirements but many primary school teachers consider them important enough to record.

It may be helpful in thinking about recording curriculum achievements to look again at Figure 1, which illustrates the assessment process. There are various types of evidence and ways of recording to consider. Not all the evidence a teacher collects in the classroom of what children say, do or produce will, or indeed should, be included in a profile. From the raw data the teacher has to make decisions about what is significant and what needs to be selected and retained. Some indication of how these judgements have been made should be included in the profile. The selected and retained evidence should comprise the core of the curriculum achievements included in the profile. The difficulty of making these decisions about what is significant should not be underestimated, particularly in terms of deciding whether evidence indicates a child has achieved a particular level in an attainment target. Some teachers find it easier to talk about children *working towards* a particular level rather than being certain that the level has been achieved. This deserves considerable attention during staff discussions and collaborative classroom work. The next step involves summarizing the evidence in some way. However, the value and usefulness of these summary sheets (indicating attainment target levels achieved) are dependent on the quality of decisions and judgements made when collecting, selecting and retaining significant evidence. The DES also requires teachers to produce a summative report at the end of each year and key stage, indicating profile component and subject levels of achievement, and this should also be an element of the profile, although some might argue the least useful.

What format should a profile have?

The format for recording and presenting the contents of profiles may include the following.

> a.   Children's accounts including personal records and statements, logbooks, journals and diaries and self-assessment records. The first two categories can be written in free prose, children have some choice over the contents although the topic may be chosen by the teacher, and children are encouraged to 'own' these and confide in them. The third category of self-assessment records could be expressed in the form of a grid of criteria, pro forma or pictorial chart against which children can assess themselves.
>
> Because these personal accounts are owned and controlled to a large extent by the child, the difficulty of teacher subjectivity in commenting on children's personal qualities is reduced in significance. There is often an opportunity for teachers to comment on the child's personal statements and self-assessments, thus achieving a balance between child and teacher comment. However, children may, and do, comment on the teacher's comments if these are considered to be inaccurate or unfair. In some schools this aspect is dealt with as an open letter from the teacher to the child. Sometimes, parents/carers are also invited to write a letter to their child, identifying achievements and this is also included in the profile.
>
> b.   Teacher-contributions, perhaps presented in the form of a Statements of Attainment (SoA) list, skills and concept criterion check-lists, grids or comment banks. However, some opportunity for open comment on the child is often also provided. The ILEA Primary Language Record provides an excellent example of what the teacher's contribution might contain. Again there is a trade-off between the time taken to complete such records by the teacher and the preservation of child individuality in the resulting document.

There are numerous examples of profiles that have been trialled in primary schools, which provide a useful starting point for a school discussion about a profile format. Although these are generally not published, schools are often prepared to share their ideas with others through informal contacts.

Bibliography

Broadfoot, P. (1986) *Profiles and Records of Achievement.* London: Holt.

DES (1984) *Records of Achievement.* London: HMSO.

DES (1988) *Records of Achievement: Report of the National Evaluation of Pilot Schemes (PRAISE Project).* London: HMSO.

Hitchcock, G. (1986) *Profiles and Profiling.* Longman.

ILEA (1988) *Primary Language Record: Handbook for Teachers.* London: Centre for Language in Primary Education.

ILEA (1990) *Patterns of Learning: The Primary Language Record and the National Curriculum.* London: Centre for Language in Primary Education.

IMPLEMENTING AND EVALUATING PROFILING

Unit B1

Analysing and Evaluating Existing Record-keeping

Aims

To analyse the school's existing record system in relation to summative and formative assessment.

Introduction

In this unit you are asked to examine the recording system in your class or school to determine whether it offers features of formative assessment. In other words, does the record help teachers to plan the learning programme for the child? If you are unclear about the distinction between formative and summative assessment, then it is suggested you tackle Unit B1b. That unit argues for the benefits of formative assessment in addition to summative statements of attainment.

Method

1   Write a list of criteria for evaluating your own records. You may find the ideas in the *Background information* helpful.

2   Using the criteria chosen, examine the record-keeping in your own class and/or school.

Which of your records show the experiences children have had?

Which of your records indicate what children have gained from experiences?

3   Records could be grouped according to these elements:

A summary record, class records, individual children's records, children's own records and samples of children's work (see *Background information*).

Which of these are included in your records?

What additional elements are included in your records?

3   Take each item in the recording system (check-list, report etc.) and decide how much **formative** information the record provides.

How is the record kept: daily, weekly, termly, yearly?

Who receives the information?

How is the teacher able to act on the information?

Is the child involved in the recording?

Follow-up

On the basis of the summative/formative analysis, review your current procedures.

List those procedures which you will maintain.

List procedures which might be discontinued.

List additional recording methods you may introduce.

Choose a new recording method to try out over the next few weeks with a small group of children. What implications does the method have for your classroom management? How useful is the information you record for informing future work with individual children?

Background information

Criteria for evaluation Do the records give the necessary factual information? Do they tell you what you need to know about outside agencies (Health, Social Services)? Do they tell you about curriculum achievements? Are children's interests and out-of-school achievements recorded? Do you need to know more about the work children have covered in school? Do the records include *evidence* of any kind? Is the record useful and easily understood?

Types of record   Clift (1981) carried out a survey of schools and the record systems which they used. He gives a list of the kinds of internal records he found in schools. These are categorized as:

1.   **A summary record** filled in at the end of each term or year. Such records were used:

    a.   to pass on information to the next class or teacher;

    b.   to keep the headteacher informed of pupils' progress (particularly in large schools);

    c.   to act as a report to parents or as a basis for writing reports to parents.

2.   **Class records** were kept more fully by those teachers who saw their teaching role in terms of organizing a whole class of children. Ticks, marks and grades were the basic methods of indicating assessments of pupils' progress. These records were kept in mark books or class lists.

3.   **Individual pupil records** were principally kept by those teachers who saw children as individual learners. A record sheet was kept for each child and usually contained considerable detail about that child's strengths and weaknesses, and had information added frequently (i.e. daily or weekly).

4.   **Pupils' own records**: Children in some schools were encouraged to keep their own records of work done. The form that these took ranged from charts kept in the back of pupils' own exercise books and individual assignment sheets to wall charts used by the whole class (see Unit B6b).

5.   **Samples of pupils' work**: Teachers in some schools kept samples of work throughout a child's school career as a measure of progress. Methods of selecting work varied from a sample taken at random throughout the year to the setting of prescribed exercises on a regular basis perhaps once or twice a term. In some cases the children themselves were responsible for the selection (see Units 6b, c and d).

Bibliography

Black, H. and Dockerell, W. B. (1980) *Diagnostic Assessment in Secondary Schools*. Edinburgh: SCRE.

Clift, P. (1981) *Record-keeping in Primary Schools.* London: Macmillan.

Summative and Formative Approaches to Record-keeping

Aims

To clarify the distinctions between *formative*, *summative* and *diagnostic* assessment.

To help teachers to see the limitations of summative assessment and the value of formative assessment in the planning process.

Introduction

The TGAT Report, which set out the model for assessment in the National Curriculum, recommended that assessment should be both formative and summative. The meaning of these terms needs to be made clear. *Summative assessment* is the traditional 'end-of-course test or examination' variety, whereby a final grade or comment is given about the learner's total achievement. This gives what is known as *feedback*. Feedback tends to be in the form of a grade without comments; assessment takes place at the end of learning when there is no time to take action.

Formative assessment, on the other hand, gives *feedforward*. Formative assessment is the judgement which enables the teacher and the learner to know what needs to be done next. Formative assessment occurs, not at the end of the learning programme, but during it, and is a continuous process. As TGAT states, *some* summative assessment is required, notably at the end of key stages and particularly at 16 in the GCSE examination, which is the end of statutory schooling.

However, TGAT's main recommendation is that the *feedforward* effects of formative assessment should be developed:

> *so that the positive achievements of a pupil may be recognised and discussed and the appropriate next steps planned.*

(TGAT, 1988, para 23)

Method

1   A well-known technique of formative assessment is miscue analysis of children's reading. Choose a child whom you know 'as a reader' and write a summative record of him/her as a reader. Then carry out a miscue analysis on his/her reading. The miscue analysis technique is described in, for example, the *ILEA Primary Language Record Handbook* (ILEA, 1988, pp. 61–3).

Examine what you have written about the child as a reader.

What are the differences between the two accounts?

2   In doing the miscue analysis, what information have you recorded about the learner which helps with planning the next stage of the child's reading?

Follow-up

Compare your findings with those of other teachers who have done this task.

Consider how the information obtained through miscue analysis could be best recorded and retained.

What strategies of classroom management would allow you to carry out this kind of assessment as part of on-going classroom work?

Background information

Formative assessment is closely related to the curriculum planning process. It is the means by which we make judgements about the next stage in the learning process. On the other hand, **summative assessment** gives no specific indication of what the next stage in learning should be. A classic example of summative assessment is the standardized reading test, which offers a reading quotient or reading age, but gives no information about the reader's strategies, skills or problems.

Summative assessment might be done by completing an assessment record check-list at the end of the year. This information may, of course, be transmitted to another teacher who may take it into account in her planning for the following year; in this case the assessment is formative. However, such a procedure clearly has less impact on the learning context than if the assessment is carried out by the teacher who is planning the next stage of the child's learning. In fact, Clift (1981, p. 20) shows how many infant and primary school teachers found that the summative records they had completed at the end of the year were never referred to by the receiving school or teachers. Naturally, the primary teachers were most dispirited by this. When the teachers in the receiving school were consulted about why they did not refer to the records sent by the partner school, the reply was often that they did not find the check-list information useful in their curriculum planning.

What evidence is there of the value of formative assessment?   Black and Dockerell (1980) demonstrate that in secondary schools both parents and pupils rank formative assessment strongly and that, where teachers put formative assessment to the top of their list, they find that they have not previously put great stress on individual feedback of learning problems.

Formative and diagnostic assessment

One type of formative assessment is sometimes known as 'diagnostic assessment'. This term has tended to be used to refer to the kind of assessment required when the learner is having difficulties and an explanation needs to be given for the difficulties so that 'remedial' provision can be made. The diagnosis would often be carried out by a specialist in assessment, such as an educational psychologist, who would then report back to the teacher the results of the enquiry, perhaps with a suggested remedial programme. Such diagnostic work may take place through the use of a particular form of a specialized test. A criticism of this form of diagnostic assessment by the educational psychologist is that it tends to lead to a remedial programme that is tightly targeted towards some known deficiency, such as lack of knowledge of phonics in reading. This can often be detached from the main activities of the children in the class and be difficult for the teacher to integrate into her teaching.

It is unfortunate that the term *diagnostic* has been exclusively associated with educational psychologists. This implies that diagnosis can only be carried out by a specialist in a situation removed from the classroom context and that the teacher may not be able to make such judgements. TGAT makes clear that diagnosis should not be the sole province of the psychologists, but that it is part of formative assessment which can, and should, be carried out by teachers:

> *We do not see the boundary between formative and diagnostic purposes as being sharp or clear. If an assessment designed in formative terms is well matched to the pupil, it is likely to provide some information which will help in the diagnosis of strengths and weaknesses. Some assessments of this kind will be of value as indicators of learning problems which require further investigation. Further diagnostic investigations would, however, often involve the use of specialist tests of relevance only to a limited set of circumstances and pupils ... Furthermore, a detailed diagnostic report on every pupil would lead to an excess of information and hence be counter-productive. We recommend that the basis of the national assessment system be essentially formative, but designed also to indicate where there is need for more detailed diagnosis.*

(TGAT, 1988, para 27)

The principle behind formative assessment is that the teacher should make judgements about the learner in a way which informs her, or other teachers, about the ways in which the child's learning can be improved: what should be done next. Diagnostic assessment is part of this process. Miscue analysis of children's reading is a good example of the way in which a teacher can gain diagnostic information about the child's learning.

The teacher, then, should see diagnostic assessment as part of her normal classroom assessment and teaching, such that she can adjust the child's learning activity within her own provision for the class.

In conclusion, formative assessment which is diagnostic should initially be undertaken:

a.   by the class-teacher, not the specialist;

b.   in the classroom context;

c.   with all children, not just those with learning difficulties.

Bibliography

Clift, P. (1981) *Record-Keeping in Primary Schools.* London: Macmillan.

TGAT (1988) *A Report.* London: DES.

ILEA(1988) *The Primary Language Record Handbook.* London: Centre for Language in Primary Education.

Evaluating Strategies for Record-keeping

Aims

To explore which strategies successfully enable record-keeping to be part of a realistic classroom routine.

Introduction

Effective record-keeping is useful, but time-consuming. If it is not to add excessively to the teacher's workload, and if it is to reflect aspects of process as well as product, time must be found in the class for building record-keeping into the fabric of the school day.

Method

1   As a staff, review your current record-keeping procedures (analysed in Unit B1a). Note when each kind of record is usually undertaken–in class with the child, at lunchtime, after school, etc.

2   As time is usually cited as the main problem, there is a need to investigate how time is spent in class. Keep a diary for a week and note the main constraints on your time in class. Which aspects of your work take up a lot of your time? It may be useful to observe each other in the classroom for this.

3   Discuss ways of making more space and time for working with individuals. Compare your ideas with those given in the background information below.

4   Review the forms of records kept. Some forms of record are too time-consuming to be functional. Complex tick sheets based on attainment targets in the National Curriculum which require another sheet as a key to tell you what to tick are not particularly useful, whereas jotted notes based on observations gathered over several weeks and reviewed at half-term might be easier to make and more informative.

Follow-up

Share as a staff any useful changes you have made in classroom organization which have facilitated record-keeping.

Spend time in each other's classrooms to look for models of different practice. If possible, arrange visits to other schools to share good practice.

Try keeping a small notebook in your hand at all times to make jottings about children which can be then transferred to a main file. In nursery and reception classes it is worth hanging a notebook near the sand and water, home corner and construction toys so that jottings can be made as you move around.

Background information

A well-organized classroom can free the teacher to focus on groups and individuals for detailed analysis. Teachers have been observed to spend a great deal of time on non-skiiled and unnecessary tasks such as handing out paper and pencils, which children can often do themselves. It is desirable for the teacher to be freed from some of the routine 'house-keeping' tasks in order to work in depth with individuals.

The following are suggested areas for consideration:

–reviewing organization of resources so that children can find and replace necessary resources independently without asking for the teacher's help.

–planning blocks of work over the whole day, or several days depending on the age of the children, so that children know what they are to do next without necessarily asking.

–encouraging the children to respect time when you as the teacher are involved with individuals. Children can be encouraged to go on to another activity if the teacher is busy, and turn to her for help when she is free.

–having clear learning aims. For example, if the children's maths task is to 'do the next page of their maths workbook', it is likely that the teacher will spend the session trouble-shooting maths problems which may not have been planned for, as thirty children encounter different problems. By contrast, the teacher who has planned that some children will be working on investigations on capacity in the water tray, while others are continuing with a known and familiar number task already introduced, is free to focus on a group of children playing Dienes game in base three and to assess their understanding prior to the introduction of tens and units.

–involving children in planning their own learning patterns. They will be more likely to work independently if they have ownership of the tasks in which they are engaged

–meeting individual needs in planning. If given tasks are carefully matched to the needs of the children, it is less likely that children will be 'stuck, miss!'.

–using support from other people wisely. Parents are often used to hear reading with individuals. It might be preferable to ask a parent to supervise a group of children engaged in a practical activity instead, thus relieving the teacher of the responsibility for that group and making it easier to focus attention on particular children.

–teach the children to mount their own work ready for display.

The programmes of study and non-statutory guidance in the National Curriculum document contain some useful comments and examples of successful classroom practice.

Bibliography

Galton, M., Simon, B. and Croll, P. (1980) *Inside the Primary School*. London: Routledge and Kegan Paul.

ILEA (1990) *Patterns of Learning*. Wells: Open Books.

Mortimore, P., Sammons, P., Stoll, L., Lewis, D. and Ecob, R. (1988) *School Matters*. Wells: Open Books.

Unit B2

Teachers' *Pictures* of Children

Aims

To examine in greater depth the pictures we have of individual children in the classroom.

Introduction

As teachers we rapidly form pictures of individual children in our classroom. The information we draw upon to construct these images comes from a variety of sources. Sometimes it comes from scrutiny of a child's past records or perhaps from a child's reputation developed lower down the school. Children in first meetings with their teachers communicate a great deal of information about themselves in various ways through verbal and non-verbal behaviour. Alongside these pictures expectations about behaviour and ability are also formed. These images and expectations harden very quickly.

Whatever the sources of the information, studies of first encounters have stressed the speed with which teachers reach conclusions about children with whom they are interacting. Research also suggests that sometimes these images are strong and stereotyped and persist, in spite of evidence to the contrary. We tend to believe, as teachers, that we are able to give an independent, objective and realistic picture of the children we interact with daily. How sure are we, however, that this is so? How confident are we that we are not overlooking evidence which is directly in front of our eyes, or that our judgement is not coloured by perhaps unacknowledged beliefs about the nature of children and the family backgrounds from which they come?

Method

1   Select three children from your class. Choose one child with whom you have an easy relationship, one with whom the relationship is more difficult and a third in your class whom you feel you know least well. Write a brief pen-portrait of each of them.

The portrait can take any form but you might include comments on a child's effort and attainment as well as notes on his/her social development and general behaviour in class.

You should consider yourself as the sole audience for this task. Do not write with anyone else in mind. Complete this part of the task before you go on to the questions in the next section. If you scan the questions first it may well influence what you write in the portraits.

2   When you have completed the task carefully examine the portraits in the ways suggested below:

    a.   What are the sexes of the children? If you chose more boys than girls or vice versa, what were the reasons for this?

    b.   Scrutinize the comments you have made on *attainment* and identify the evidence on which you are basing these comments.

    c.   Examine the comments you have made about *effort* in a similar manner. How do you know the extent or degree to which these particular children are making an effort?

    d.   If you have made any classifications according to *ability*, for example, *bright*, *slow learner*, *remedial*, clarify the reasons for your use of these words.

    e.   Carefully examine the *language* of each report. How many words have a negative connotation and how many are positive?

f.   If you have used words like *mature, sensible, moody, open, responsible* clarify exactly what these words mean to you.

g.   Have you mentioned the *home background* of the child and are you using ideas about social class, race or status of family, for example, single-parent, as reasons for attainment or effort?

Follow-up

At the end of this task it might be useful to reflect on how well you actually know the children in your class and how objective the judgements you are making about them might be.

How did your judgements about their personalities, attributes and attainments come to be made?

In what ways might it be appropriate to change the language you use in describing children for recording purposes?

Are there gaps in your knowledge about the children and, if so, how might they be filled?

Background information

The image we have of a child is sometimes built unknowingly on what we have heard about the child before he or she reaches our class. Some children, as they move through school, acquire an image that precedes them. Sometimes the image is positive and on other occasions negative. It is often fed by staffroom conversations where *difficult* children are talked about, perhaps with reference to their siblings and the family from which they come. When we receive the child for the first time it is difficult not to be influenced by this information.

Family background and social class are especially important and may affect a teacher's perceptions of a child even before the child becomes a full-time pupil, or at least very shortly afterwards.

Rist (1970) in his study of an urban ghetto school in the United States found that the images teachers had of children were built up very quickly during first encounters in the first year of infant school. He noted that the children were divided into groups within eight days of their first entry to school. The groups were formed of those children who were expected to learn and those who were not. Expectations were based not on measured ability or performance but on the children's speech, appearance and social background. The teachers had formed an ideal image of what was necessary for academic success and this *typification* affected a child's subsequent contact with the teacher and his/her future in the school. In this way children tend to achieve a 'track record' which affects the way they see themselves and the way they are seen by their teachers and by other children.

As the year proceeds other factors may come into play. Becker (1952) suggested that teachers have a picture of what constitutes an 'ideal' child against which the children they teach are measured. If children do not conform to this ideal, then teachers may be unable to see other positive attributes that they possess. This notion was echoed in the work of Sharp and Green (1975), who found that in an infant classroom some children were taught to a lesser degree because they were considered by their teachers not to have been socialized adequately into the skills required for learning. King (1978) found that this process of typification started on the very first day of school.

As teachers we tend to believe that, while this happens elsewhere, it does not happen in our own school. But the influences at work are very subtle and an image of a child based on erroneous information can be built up very quickly and often without our realization. This image can then strongly influence our expectations about a child's ability and attainment with lasting effects. In Unit B2b you can examine the picture you have drawn of your three children in an attempt to ascertain the degree of your objectivity in relation to each.

Bibliography

Becker, H. S. (1952) 'Social class variations in the teacher pupil relationship', *Journal of Educational Sociology* 25 (8) in Hammersley, M. (ed.) (1986) *Case Studies in Classroom Research.* Milton Keynes: Open University Press, pp. 451–65.

King, R. (1978) *All Things Bright and Beautiful?* Chichester: Wiley.

Rist, R. (1970) 'Student social class and teacher expectations', *Harvard Educational Review* 40 (3) in Hammersley, M. (ed.) (1986) *Case Studies in Classroom Research.* Milton Keynes: Open University Press, pp. 411–51.

Sharp, R. and Green, W. A. (1975) *Education and Social Control.* London: Routledge and Kegan Paul.

Using Research Findings to Improve Teachers' *Pictures* of Children

Aims

To reconsider the picture we have of individual children in the classroom in the light of evidence from research sources and to consider the degree of subjectivity or objectivity employed in making judgements about children.

Introduction

In the last unit you drew pen-portraits of three children in your classroom and then examined the portraits you had drawn in greater depth. An attempt was made to show that teachers have images of children which are not always objective but are sometimes based on cultural stereotypes of class and family background. These stereotypes may also include race and gender. In this task we are attempting to extend this analysis further and to consider the degree to which these stereotypes may influence the assessments we make of individual children.

An additional element to come into play in this context is the phenomenon known as the *halo effect*. Once children have acquired a positive image in one or two areas of the curriculum there is a tendency to view them as operating equally well in all areas of the curriculum. From this belief we tend to have positive expectations about the children's performance. Rosenthal and Jacobson (1968) in a well-publicized piece of research outlined the effect of such *self-fulfilling prophecies.* In their study, teachers and children produced the kind of results which tallied with the teacher's, in this case, inaccurately conceived expectations of the performance of a class.

Method

Read the *Background information* and reconsider the three pen-portraits you wrote in the last unit (B2a), in the light of the evidence given, using the questions below.

    a.   How far has your selection of pupils been affected by their gender?

    b.   Is the pupil you interact with least a girl?

    c.   How would you rate your selected children on a scale of 1 to 5 for attractiveness?

            Child 1   attractive 1 2 3 4 5 unattractive

            Child 2   attractive 1 2 3 4 5 unattractive

            Child 3   attractive 1 2 3 4 5 unattractive

    d.   How far did *speech* play a part in the selection of the three pupils?

    e.   How accurate are your labels of ability? How well do you know your pupils in all areas of the curriculum?

    f.   How accurate are the words you use in describing your pupils? How far are they free of stereotypical images and supportable by independent evidence?

Follow-up

At the end of this task you might like to consider to what degree more detailed observations and recording of children's achievements could help diagnose their weaknesses or highlight their achievements. How far would children's own perspectives help provide a more accurate profile of their classroom experiences?

Background information

Gender issues Research in classrooms suggests that, on the whole, teachers prefer boys to girls and that boys are more likely than girls to be teachers' favourites. Stanworth (1983), for example, found that when asked to name their favourite pupils women teachers were likely to opt for boys twice as often as they opted for girls while male teachers were ten times as likely to opt for boys as for girls.

Pye (1988) found girls far more likely to be 'hidden' in the classroom, more faceless and less likely to be well known by the teacher. Keddie (1977) too found that teachers asked questions of boys as individuals but of girls as a group. They tended to know boys more as *individuals*.

Appearance and speech A number of studies of individual differences have suggested that children's personality, physical attractiveness and speech characteristics all affect the teacher's response to individual children. Dion (1972) found that physical attractiveness bred positive expectations on the part of the teachers for children's academic performance. Eltis (1976) in his research with Australian teachers demonstrated that children's accents exerted a wide-ranging influence on their judgements about children: those with Standard English accents were considered to be of higher ability.

For most of us it seems it is initially easier to like, and to have positive expectations of, children who are particularly attractive. Likewise we tend to underrate children whose language we find difficult to follow. Although there has been an acceptance of regional accents, there still appears to be a hierarchy of dialects in the classroom and these often form the basis of beliefs about children's ability.

Ability labels Labels such as *bright* or *slow* are often a means of dividing children into manageable groups for teaching situations. Indeed, the grouping of children often revolves around their performance in one curriculum area such as language or maths. The terms themselves, however, may mask important individual differences. What is applicable in one area is not always so in others. In addition the 'halo' effect may come into operation whereby a child who is achieving in one area of the curriculum comes to be perceived as achieving in other areas. Likewise a child who is under-achieving may be perceived as failing in all areas. These labels, if communicated to the children, may evoke the expected behaviours as children produce the work expected of them.

Language used The words we select to describe others often carry emotional connotations and words which are positive like 'careful' become negative with only a slight change of emphasis. *Careful* can be *miserly* in a different context.

Likewise many words used to describe children are vague, with meanings that are difficult to assess without information about the context in which they were written. When can a child be considered *mature*, for example? We might all have different ideas about what constitutes maturity. Some people would undoubtedly claim that, by definition, children are immature. How sure are we that we are conveying an accurate meaning? Would we use the same words if we were communicating this information to others: parents/carers, for example? If not how would we explain the discrepancies?

Some words have gender associations. Jones (1981) found that *quiet, industrious, mature, responsible, spiteful, vicious, cunning* and *moody* were more likely to be used to describe girls, whereas *noisy, cheeky, boisterous, aggressive, open* and *direct* were adjectives applied to boys. How far can we be sure that we are not seeing individual children in the light of their gender?

Social class and status of family Background frequently plays an important part in teachers' descriptions of children. Children from 'broken homes' or from 'one-parent families' are often labelled as experiencing similar difficulties although they are very often in very different circumstances. The description *broken home* has emotional connotations which suggest pain and trauma. This may well be true, but not all one-parent families are in this category and some broken homes may be well on the way to 'repair' by the time the children enter your class. Likewise children from working-class backgrounds are less likely to be deemed 'ready to learn' than their middle-class counterparts (Sharp and Green, 1975).

Expectations that we have about ourselves, and expectations that others have about us, are very powerful determinants of behaviour. The image of a child is frequently created through the interaction between child and teacher in the classroom. Schmuck and Schmuck (1979) have outlined this process very well. They suggest that children who feel secure and confident in the classroom will behave in a friendly and supportive way in relationships. Other children and the teacher will react positively to this behaviour and so reinforce the image the child has of him/herself. Negative behaviour is likely to work in a similar manner. In this way, through the circular interpersonal process between teacher and child, self-images are built up and become self-perpetuating.

Bibliography

Dion, K. *et al.* (1972) 'What is good is beautiful?', *Journal of Personality and Social Psychology* 24, pp. 285–90.

Eltis, K.J. (1976) *The ascription of attitudes to pupils by teachers with particular reference to the influence of voice in the process.* Macquarie University, Sydney. PhD. Thesis.

Jones, R. (1981) *Inside the Classroom.* Milton Keynes: Open University. E205, No. 10 Block 2.

Keddie, N. (1971) 'Classroom knowledge', in Young, M.F.D. (ed.) *Knowledge and Control: New Directions in the Sociology of Education.* London: Collier Macmillan.

Pye, J. (1988) *Invisible Children.* Milton Keynes: Open University Press.

Rosenthal, R. and Jacobson, L. (1968) *Pygmalion in the Classroom.* London: Holt, Rinehart and Winston.

Schmuck, R. A. and Schmuck, P. A. (1979) *Group Processes in the Classroom.* Dubuque, Iowa: Wm C Brown.

Sharp, R. and Green, W. A. (1975) *Education and Social Control.* London: Routledge and Kegan Paul.

Stanworth, M. (1983) *Gender and Schooling – A Study of Sexual Divisions in the Classroom.* London: Hutchinson.

Improving Children's Self-image

Aims

To investigate children's self-image in the classroom with a view to enhancing self-esteem.

Introduction

Children's experience of school, their feelings about life in classrooms and their own self-image as pupils remain relatively hidden phenomena in school life. Little has been written or explored in this area. This may be partly due to the labelling of young people as immature and therefore unable to make reasonable judgements. Nevertheless, in classroom situations they are the 'user group' and play an active part in shaping the life of the classroom. Moreover, children's experience of the educative process, their assessments of their own performances and their understanding of classroom processes are likely to give teachers a better understanding of the relationship between teaching and learning in their classroom.

This unit and Unit B4 will focus on the contribution children can make in this area. Research suggests that children's self-images affect their performances in school (Benjamin, 1950) and that many children either have a relatively poor self-image or else seriously underestimate their ability to perform in given curriculum areas. This has been particularly true of girls, who have tended both to underestimate their ability in certain areas and to compare themselves unfavourably with boys.

Profiling may offer us a unique opportunity to work on pupil self-esteem. A number of the tasks outlined below are aimed at enhancement of self-esteem. Some of the tasks are quick and simple, others more protracted; some need teacher involvement, others do not. Select one or two from the list to try with your own children. After they have been completed you may like to consider which tasks could be recorded in a profile, and how.

Method

1 Choose a small number of children to whom you can talk on a one-to-one basis. You could focus on the three children whom you chose for the pen-portraits although this is not essential.

No particular focus is suggested for this activity since an important aspect would be to acknowledge success which is not necessarily connected with classroom activities. It might then be possible to help children to see how skills and interests are transferable from one area to another and for you as the teacher to build on a child's interests and achievements in making the curriculum more relevant to individual needs.

The conversation should centre on the question, 'What do you think you do well?', and should be followed up by a record being made of the outcomes. This could be in written or in pictorial forms.

Children often overlook or undervalue their particular strengths and careful probing is necessary in order to explore this question fully. Gurney (1990) suggests that when it is completed the end result could be pasted into a workbook, pinned inside a desk lid or put in a work tray. It could also form part of a pupil's profile. Unit B2d takes up this approach and explores child conferencing.

2 Devise a number of statements which can be attributed to individuals in a child's life, for example, *myself, my mother, my father, my friend, my teacher.*

Make a postbox for each person and allow the relative statements to be posted into the appropriate box with the teacher's help.

This task may allow you to probe more deeply into a child's particular self-image. Enhancement of self-image is important for us all, but some children have a particularly low self-image and this fact may often be relatively hidden. The task allows for the possibility of more in-depth conversations with parents. It also may reveal information which needs sensitive handling. You should look at Unit B8d in connection with this.

3   Take simple photographs of classroom life and use them as a basis for discussion and records. Photographs of individual children and classroom activities can be used in a variety of ways to enhance self-esteem and contribute to profiles of the children. There are some suggestions given below.

Gurney (1990) suggests that photographs carefully handled can allow children to discuss the things they dislike about themselves as well as the things they feel pleased about. However, this activity depends on a good and supportive classroom environment.

Katy Simmons (1990) demonstrates how photographs have been of major importance in recording the responses and progress of the most severely handicapped pupils of infant age and above. They not only provide a record of important classroom events but also allow for the minutiae of progress to be noted. It may well be that the children can be involved in taking the photographs themselves and thus contributing to their own profile.

4   Ask the children to draw or paint a picture of 'myself in the classroom'.

When the picture is completed it is then necessary to have some in-depth discussion in order to draw out further the feelings which have prompted the painting.

Work with children in hospitals and other more 'closed' institutions has suggested that pictures provide very strong evidence about how children feel, both about themselves and their immediate environment. Children in hospital, for example, tend to portray themselves as being dwarfed by the institution in which they find themselves. Similarly, children drawing pictures of classroom life often emphasize points which would be totally overlooked by the teacher. Even though we may inhabit the same space, our perceptions and experiences of that space may be quite different. The intention in a child formulating a profile of school life is to include items from a child's standpoint.

5   Encourage the children to record positive experiences as they happen.

This can take any form which either you or the children think desirable. It might include a brief statement by the child with some added comments about the detail of the achievement and the context in which it occurred.

The incident to be recorded may be a particular job done well, a piece of work showing personal progress, a one-off achievement in perhaps a musical or sporting event. The object would be to ensure that positive achievements were recorded for everyone, not solely those children who appear to achieve all the time. The idea of profiling is to include a proper record of the achievements of children who have not traditionally profited a great deal from their school experiences.

Gurney (1990) rightly suggests that memories of success are short-lived for both teachers and children. A system which allows children to keep a record of what they have done would allow all of them to document and celebrate their successes.

Follow-up

At the end of this unit you might like to consider the degree to which your image of a child is in accord with the child's image of him or herself.

You might also like to reflect on the enhancement of self-image and the steps the class teacher can take to facilitate this.

How can you implement these steps in your own classroom?

How could collaborative work with a colleague support this?

Many of the tasks suggested in this unit would form an important part of a child's profile. It is very easy to accumulate a good deal of data in this way but how would you select what should be retained and whose job should it be to make this decision? Should the decision be left to the child or to the teacher, or be the result of negotiation between them?

Background information

PRAISE (1988) found that pupils wanted a record of their school lives for posterity. There appears to be a strong need in all of us to look back on the important elements of our lives in some detail whether it be through the use of photographs or diaries. They are all important in the sense we make of our lives and our personal biographies. Pupils are no exception to this.

This unit has explored the idea that most people are unable to value their achievements properly. This is very noticeable with adult learners returning to full-time education after a considerable period of absence. Its origins appear rooted in early education where stress is often placed on what children cannot do rather than on their assets. With all adult returners it is possible to highlight their very considerable achievements and increase self-confidence, but the long-lasting effects of poor self-image which originate in childhood are not so easy to overcome.

Bibliography

Benjamin, J. (1950) 'Changes in relation to influences upon self-conceptualization', *Journal of Abnormal and Social Psychology* 45, pp. 573-80.

Gurney, P. (1990) 'The enhancement of personal esteem in junior classrooms', in Docking. J. (ed.) *Education and Alienation in the Junior School.* Lewes: Falmer.

Simmons, K. (1990) 'Pictures of progress', *Times Educational Supplement,* 2 February.

Conferencing with Children

Aims

To explore child conferences as a means of helping us to understand more about children and their attitudes/feelings towards school.

Introduction

A child conference is a one-to-one discussion between teacher and child in which the child is given the opportunity to share her views, take the initiative in the conversation and express what interests, motivates and concerns her. This unit deals with conferences which explore children's feelings about school and develops further the approach suggested in Unit B2c. These conferences can be extremely productive in terms of providing teachers with a 'rounded' picture. To understand the child it is necessary to encourage him/her to talk about experiences of school and to discuss the background to attitudes expressed. For example, fear of being left out of things at playtime, or a bad reading experience in a previous class can have an effect on the child's performance and happiness in school. Unit B8 explores the use of conferences to elicit aspects of the child's life outside school and these can provide teachers with different, but none the less valuable, insights into the child.

Method

1   With a colleague, or as a staff, brainstorm the sorts of things it might be useful to find out about a child as a pupil in school. Obviously these will not be the same for each child–for example, you may wish to discuss in depth if s/he has particular difficulties–but explore the range of concerns.

Your list may include:

> Does s/he like school? If not, why?
>
> What does s/he like best? Why?
>
> What is s/he good at?

What has s/he enjoyed most in the last week/term/year?

What has been least enjoyable?

Is there anything s/he feels s/he is not good at? Why?

Is there anything s/he worries about at school?

What about friends – who are his/her closest friends?

2   How might these aspects of a child's experience be built into a conference? It is best to avoid a questionnaire-type approach. Strategies for encouraging the child to talk without over-use of questioning should be used (see Unit B5c). How will you overcome the practical problem of freeing yourself to work with an individual? How much time will you allow for each child? How will you record the outcome?

3   Try a few conferences with children including these aspects.

Follow-up

Review what you have found out. Has the conference added to your knowledge of the child? Did anything that arose surprise you? Compare your findings with those in the *Background information*. What changes could you make to your practices in school and classroom organization as a result of your findings? Did you find the experience valuable enough to want to incorporate it into your teaching approach? What would need to change to allow you to build child conferences of this type into your classroom work?

Background information

Teachers trying out conferences with children through ILEA's *Primary Language Record* were often surprised by what emerged from the child's comments about school. For example:

–painful early reminiscences about learning to read in another class which helped explain current negative attitudes. Lack of parental involvement had previously been cited as a major factor, but the school's contribution had been overlooked!

–great anxiety amongst Year 6 children about going to secondary school and whether they would be 'good enough' led to teachers being more careful about making comments like 'when you get to the secondary school you won't be able to get away with that!' It also led to teachers exploring ways of making greater links with secondary schools at an earlier stage.

–children were honest about their strengths, and the teacher could ask about weaknesses too without being negative. Children were aware of their own difficulties, but they are often not openly discussed. The conferences enabled the teachers to have open discussions with children about learning difficulties, agreeing short-term targets for further development.

–one child explained his disruptive behaviour by describing how he became rigid every time he knew he was going to be asked to write, becoming so tense he could not hold his pencil, and showing a tendency to 'explode' into violence. This explanation helped the teacher support his learning difficulties, and therefore help control his frustrated (and frustrating!) behaviour.

–'boring books' were sometimes cited as reasons for children not enjoying reading, and this led schools to examine their book provision.

The examples cited above provided insights in the language area. Child conferences can reveal useful information in other areas of the curriculum. It can be nerve-racking encouraging children to talk about school openly, but the insights gained can be extremely useful, both in understanding individual children and in reviewing our own practice.

Bibliography

ILEA (1988) *The Primary Language Record: Handbook for Teachers.* London: Centre for Language in Primary Education.

Martin, T. (1986) *The Strugglers.* Milton Keynes: Open University Press.

Unit B3

Meeting Legal Requirements

Aims

To ensure that the school's record-keeping procedures allow legal requirements to be met but are not confined or constrained by them.

Introduction

Record-keeping in a school, following the 1988 Education Act, needs to have at least three purposes. First, a school must provide information to parents/carers about the achievements of their child, as already outlined in Unit A2. Second, schools must provide sufficient data about the achievements of all the children in the school to the LEA and the DES, who will be checking that the National Curriculum is being fully implemented in each school. Finally, schools must maintain the necessary records to ensure continuity without repetition. The latter records are familiar practice in primary schools and are already used both to assist the planning of individual teachers and to ensure continuity within a school. Because the situation with regard to legal requirements for recording and reporting (particularly with regard to the second two purposes) is likely to be clarified, the information available in this unit needs to be supplemented by the latest updates available from the DES and your LEA.

Method

Read the background information accompanying this unit. Consider the latest record-keeping requirements from the LEA and the DES; devise strategies whereby these can effectively be completed without committing large amounts of teacher time. Consider what record-keeping is needed to fulfil new requirements alongside current recording procedures: do the local and national requirements assist in any way in improving these? Again, it is necessary to develop effective strategies which are not over-demanding on teacher time.

Follow-up

It will be necessary to review the school's record-keeping regularly in the light of new regulations from the DES.

Background information

Unit A2 dealt with the legal requirements concerning the recording and reporting of individual children. This unit concentrates on the other aspects of the statutory requirements relating to recording. There has been some disarray within the DES over the national arrangements for reporting in compliance with the National Curriculum terms of the 1988 Act. Templates were initially sent to schools which asked heads to report on the time given to each subject in each year (Circulars 14/89 and 17/89). These were subsequently withdrawn for primary schools. Less time-consuming instruments have since been introduced. The completion of these is a legal requirement. However, they only show the coverage of National Curriculum and other subjects over a year. Furthermore, they have no connection with the specific curricular and assessment aims of particular schools. In other words, this aspect of National Curriculum recording is of a limited nature and will offer little to schools.

It is the responsibility of individual heads to collate all the information about the achievements of children in their schools and the record-keeping systems in operation will need to enable this to be done with the least possible effort. The DES document *National Curriculum Assessment Arrangements*, published in July 1990, gives information about aggregation and how AT and PC levels are to be calculated. In many situations the analysis of the levels and the collation of information may be best achieved through the use of a computer program. These arrangements require schools to report to their LEAs and for the LEAs to report to the DES.

The format in which schools will have to provide evidence of continuity and coverage of programmes of study is through schemes of work which are described in the Non-Statutory Guidance for the core subjects. Further information about this is anticipated from the DES and LEAs.

Access to Children's Records

Aims

To consider the legal requirements in terms of access to individual records.

Introduction

Circulars 14/89 and 8/90 from the DES set out the legal requirements for making information available to parents. As outlined in Unit A2, schools need to devise systems that allow them to report progress in attainment targets in each key stage. However, DES circulars also make clear what handwritten or typed material must be made available to parents on request. Computerized records, already covered by the Data Protection Act, are always open to parental inspection. It would be wise for schools and teachers to assume that all their records on pupils may be open to parental scrutiny. Teachers and heads should therefore write all their records in a clear and positive way and ensure factual accuracy of all points.

There is little point in having a record of achievement at primary level if it is not something which is shared on a regular or continual basis with parents/carers. Whilst access by teachers within a school is probably uncontroversial, children may not wish other children or non-teaching staff to see their records. Such issues are increasingly likely to surface throughout the primary years as children become aware of the differential nature of their achievements.

Method

Consider the school's policy on, first, *ownership of* and, second, *access to* records. Establish a policy which best meets the needs of children, teachers, parents and other schools.

Follow-up

Collect views from children, parents/carers with regard to the appropriateness of the school's policy on ownership and access and its effectiveness in practice. In the light of these views and of teachers' own experiences of the implementation of the policy, consider whether it needs revision.

Unit B4

Self-assessment

Making Criteria for Success Explicit to Children

Aims

To investigate how far making criteria for success explicit to children affects and enables their learning, and the assessment and recording of their learning.

Introduction

Although the teacher's general expectations regarding the quality of children's work are often well assimilated by the children, and may be reiterated before each session, it is less common for lesson plans to include an indication of the criteria to be used to evaluate success. It is even less likely that such criteria will have been made clear to children and used in both self-assessment and teacher assessment.

Method

1   Review and list the learning tasks in which your class were engaged during the last two days.

2   For each task or activity, address the following questions:

  a.   Did you have clear criteria for assessment of the task before starting?

  b.   If so, were the children aware of the criteria?

  c.   Which criteria were finally used to assess the learning, and by whom?

  d.   How far were the children involved in assessing their own achievements?

e.   Was any record kept of the children's work and learning?

f.   Was each child aware of his/her performance on each task and, if so, did the child's perception match the teacher's?

3   In small groups, compare your lists.

a.   Were the criteria for success more likely to be made explicit in some curriculum areas/tasks than others?

b.   Were some criteria more likely to be made explicit than others, for example, neatness, speed of working?

c.   Where criteria were made explicit, what effect did this have on the children's learning and the teacher's response?

4   Review your teaching plans for the next few days. Try to write clear criteria for success into the plans for one or two tasks and make these clear to the children before they start. On completion, involve the children in deciding whether the criteria have been met.

It is worth trying this exercise more than once. Your ability (and the children's ability!) to identify and focus on specific criteria will probably improve each time.

Follow-up

In groups, discuss the outcome of the sessions. Some questions you might consider are:

a.   Was having clear criteria for assessment useful to the children? Did it help you as the teacher?

b.   How easy/difficult was it to involve the children in the assessment?

c.   Did the exercise affect the quality of the children's learning? How?

d.   Were there any differences in the assessments of teacher and child? How were these resolved?

e.   How were the outcomes recorded?

From your discussions it should be possible to draw up some criteria for incorporating any useful aspects of the exercise into your teaching. What issues concerning children's self-assessment have arisen as a result of this activity? The following units (B4b, c and d) explore self-assessment in more depth.

Background information

One of the key aspects of profiling is the involvement of the child in recording his/her achievements and progress. In many schools children have been involved in discussions to review their work in process and/or on completion (see Unit A3), and it has been a natural progression from this to realize that we might involve them even earlier in the learning process. It has become common practice in some schools, for example, for children to 'brainstorm' with the teacher around the chosen topic for the term, perhaps also prioritizing areas on which they would like to focus in the term's work.

However, it is less likely that children will be clear about the learning aims for a particular session, and therefore be able to become actively involved in achieving them. There is a tendency for teachers to regard explicit aims as a type of professional secret, whilst sharing with the children their disappointment if the learning aims are not met! Sometimes children believe that they have been learning something quite different from that which the teacher had planned. Children colouring in shapes in a Maths exercise, for example, may feel it more important to prove that at seven they don't go 'over the edge' when colouring, than to demonstrate their knowledge of what properties make a shape a square rather than a triangle!

Where there has been involvement with children in making explicit the criteria for success in their learning, the children have joint ownership in the learning activity and are more likely to work in partnership with the teacher to achieve those aims. In working with children with learning difficulties, for example, having clear short-term aims for a session is known to make the successful achievement of those aims more certain. This gives a subsequent boost to the child's self-esteem, and the motivation to move on. The child still may not be able to read independently, for example, as this is a long-term aim; but she may have successfully used books to discover three interesting facts about centipedes by working collaboratively with a partner.

Children are very aware of their own strengths and weaknesses and can be very honest in conferences in evaluating their performance. By entering into a dialogue with children about the explicit aims for a session, and the criteria for success, we can involve them in taking on a greater responsibility for their own learning. This can only benefit their development and the teacher's ability to meet individual needs.

Bibliography

DES (1984) *The Curriculum from 5–16, Curriculum Matters No 2.* London: HMSO.

ILEA (1988) *The Primary Language Record: Handbook for Teachers.* London: Centre for Language in Primary Education.

Mercer, N. and Edwards, E. (1987) *Common Knowledge.* London: Methuen.

Using Children's Self-assessment

Aims

To use children's self-assessment as a tool in formative assessment.

Introduction

Formative assessment has always been a part of classroom life (see Unit B1b). Teachers constantly help with children's work and diagnose difficulties as they move around the classroom or interact with individual children. Nevertheless this has tended to be on an *ad hoc* basis with sometimes little structure or follow-up. Indeed, research (Bennett *et al.*, 1984) suggests that, although teachers know that children are failing to complete the work successfully, they are often unaware of the precise nature of a child's difficulties. This has led, it is suggested, to a mismatch between child and task.

The activities below are designed to encourage children to reflect on their work after they have completed it. This may then provide an agenda for teacher and child to review the task and to identify difficulties. It may not always be possible to do this; but it might be particularly profitable to do it with children experiencing difficulties, as well as children who find tasks comparatively easy.

The tasks are adapted from Bray and Lloyd Jones (1986). You should select one approach from the list given and try it out with a small group of children. Once again you could involve the three children you originally selected (Unit B2a) in order to provide a more in-depth picture of their classroom performance, or you could choose others.

Method

1   When the child has completed a piece of work ask him/her to complete a simple pro forma along the lines suggested below:

By doing the work I learnt............

When doing this work the difficulties I had were..........

I think I could improve if...............

The things I enjoyed about this work were.................

I think my standard of work is.......................

With very young children it would be necessary to complete this through conversation and to modify the questions appropriately.

2   Ask the child to describe his/her interest in the work either orally or in writing.

This is a simpler method of gaining insight into children's reactions to a project. It could be done in a variety of ways: it could be a simple conversation between teacher and child or it could be a conversation between a group of children which was recorded. This could be done with or without the teacher's presence, bearing in mind that the teacher is likely to alter the course of the conversation in both positive and negative ways.

3   Record a piece of dance or drama with video equipment and then analyse it with the child/children.

Creative work is far more difficult to assess than other areas of the curriculum. Nevertheless it is important for self-assessment that these areas be tackled as well. This could be done on special occasions through the use of a video camera.

Analysis by audience and participants after a particular piece of creative work is already a part of classroom life. Nevertheless it is not a technique which is widely utilized. Indeed, in many instances it may be inappropriate. It is sometimes useful to evaluate performance in a structured way. This can be done through dialogue alone or, if there is any access to video equipment, the recording of dance or drama and its subsequent analysis.

4   Develop the analysis of the child's work in more depth using the example given below, or one of your own choosing.

Self-analysis, after the child has completed a task, may take the form of a simple sheet containing general statements as in task 1. Alternatively it may be more structured in a form which is already prepared by the teacher prior to the setting of the task.

Here is an example of a mathematical task for Year 3 children, who were required to measure pieces of wood 10 cm long to make a box. At the end of the task they were asked to complete the following questions:

Checking your skills–When measuring the lengths did you:

a.   Choose to use a ruler, tape-measure or something else?

b.   Choose the correct scale (centimetres not inches)?

c.   Take care to place the beginning of the scale exactly against the left-hand end of the wood?

d.   Keep the ruler or tape close to the edge of the wood or exactly on top of it while measuring?

e.   Read the number nearest but to the left of the end?

f.   Mark the wood carefully using a pencil?

g.   Check your measuring carefully?

Now compare your piece of wood with this one (provided). Were you correct?

If the one you cut is a different length, why do you think they are different?

Follow-up

At this point you might like to reflect on the information you have gained from the task(s) you have completed. How is this likely to affect your planning of tasks in the future

    a.   for the whole class?

    b.   for individual children who have experienced difficulties?

How could the results of this kind of self-assessment be appropriately recorded?

How could your practice be changed to encourage more self-assessment?

If you already operate a negotiated curriculum, in which children are involved in planning, you might like to consider the ways in which you already engage in formative assessment of this kind and the ways in which you could develop your approach.

Discuss the extent to which your colleagues have been able to encourage children's self-assessment and how they have recorded the outcomes.

What contribution can self-assessment make to a child's profile?

Background information

Teachers have often questioned children's abilities to assess themselves in a learning situation. Fairbairn (1988) and others have found that, in fact, children are likely to know better than teachers how hard they have tried and the degree to which they have experienced difficulty. In addition, children's self-assessments are likely to provide teachers with feedback on the matching of task to child as well as to the appropriateness of the task in general. In this way self-assessment can have a marked effect on the planning of the learning environment.

Self-assessment may also record not just the extent of children's knowledge but also their understanding of what they have learnt. It allows for the evaluation of subject-specific skills and cross-curricular skills. It could take some of the burden from teachers by including the child in the assessment process. Fairbairn notes that the following ideas should be taken into consideration when making judgements about the effectiveness of a self-evaluation programme:

1.   the purposes of self-assessment must be made clear to pupils;

2.   the language and criteria used in assessment must be intelligible to them;

3.   pupils must feel that the self-assessment is more than just a dialogue with themselves. It must be commented upon and acted upon within the school.

(Fairbairn, 1988, p. 60)

Bibliography

Bennett, N. *et al.* (1984) *The Quality of Pupil Learning Experiences.* London: Lawrence Erlbaum Associates.

Black, H. (1986) 'Assessment for learning' in Nuttall, D.L. (ed.) *Assessing Educational Achievement.* Lewes: Falmer.

Black, H. D. and Dockerell, W. B. (1984) *Criterion-referenced Assessment in the Classroom.* Edinburgh: SCRE.

Bray, E. 'Profiling' in Lloyd Jones, R. and Bray, E. (eds) (1988) *Assessment from Principles to Action.* London: Macmillan.

Fairbairn, D.J. (1988) 'New approaches to recording and reporting achievement', in Murphy, R. and Torrance, H. (eds) *The Changing Face of Educational Assessment.* Milton Keynes: Open University Press.

Satterley, D. (1989) 'Profiles and Records of Achievement', in *Assessment in Schools.* London: Blackwell.

Encouraging Children's Self-assessment as Well as Teacher Assessment

Aims

To plan a piece of work using both self-assessment and teacher assessment.

Introduction

In the last unit (B4b) we investigated the possibility of the children reflecting on their work after they had completed the task. Although this is a valuable exercise, reflection before the task is begun and negotiation between teacher and child may result in the teaching and learning aims becoming clearer. Evidence seems to suggest that, for some tasks, specified goals help the children in self-assessment. These goals can be set by the children, by the teachers or by negotiation between the two. Much will depend on the age and ability of the children taking part in the exercise. It may be easier to commence with teacher-directed goals but as the children become more skilled and more autonomous in their working they may take on much of the responsibility for goal-setting themselves.

Planning and goal-setting can take a variety of forms and fit into a variety of classroom settings. It would be interesting to link this area of profiling with the negotiated curriculum where children and teachers are involved jointly in the planning process. In addition, goal-setting can form an important part of a more formal classroom setting where an individual piece of work in a named curriculum area or topic work could be planned, with its aims clearly agreed and the criteria for assessment by both children and teachers clarified.

Method

1   Working with an individual child or a small group of children, identify a piece of work to be undertaken, specify the goals for the work and the method to be employed.

When the work is completed get the children to evaluate how they planned the work, what preparation was needed and what difficulties were encountered.

2   Break down a particular unit of learning into its component parts before you set it for the children. When they have finished the task evaluate the component parts to understand precisely what the children had difficulty with. For this task you could experiment with Bloom's (1971) categories given in the *Background information* and then attempt your own categories to aid formative assessment.

3   After a task has been completed examine the introduction you gave to the task, any explanation you gave, and the way in which the elements of the task were ordered.

4   Working with a group of children, allow them to specify their own goals for an individual task. When the work is done, review the task with them. How far have they reached their goals? How far are their goals different from yours?

Follow-up

Review what you have done so far about self-assessment and consider its implications for your classroom work.

Have any other issues arisen about how the outcomes of self-assessment might be recorded?

Self-assessment is given further attention in the following unit (B4d).

Background information

Bloom suggested the following classifications for considering children's learning:

a. **Knowledge of terms**   These are the specific terms that the child is required to recognize at any particular stage. Beyond recognition of terms there may be required the ability to decide whether the term is being used correctly or incorrectly.

b. **Knowledge of facts**   This is relatively self-explanatory but it may be helpful to decide what information a child needs to know in order to perform the task in question.

c. **Knowledge of rules and principles**   Investigate the rules that the particular task you have set demands knowledge of.

d. **Skill in using processes and procedures**   This often demands following a process in an appropriate sequence.

e. **Ability to make translations**   This procedure is used when children are asked to write things in their own words, for example.

f. **Ability to make applications**   This procedure is used when children are asked to apply rules or procedures in new situations.

Bennett *et al.* (1984) have demonstrated that teachers frequently set tasks which are not ideally suited to all the learners in the classroom. Bloom (1971) suggests that the quality of teaching then needs examining. Children often put good explanations at the top of their list of good teaching skills (Wragg and Wood, 1984).

Bibliography

Bennett, N. *et al.* (1984) *The Quality of Pupil Learning Experiences.* London: Lawrence Erlbaum Associates.

Bloom, B. S. *et al.* (1971) *Handbook on Formative and Summative Evaluation of Student Learning.* New York: McGraw-Hill.

Wragg, E. C. and Wood, E. K. (1984) 'Teachers' first encounters with their classes', in Wragg, E. (ed.) *Classroom Teaching Skills.* London: Croom Helm.

Using Self-assessment to Enable Children to Identify Progress

Aims

To utilize profiles to enable children to identify the progress they have made and to stimulate further success.

Introduction

Research into self-image suggests that children underperform because they underestimate their own achievements. It may not be solely low self-confidence that is underlying this phenomenon but also a lack of self-knowledge and inability to think critically. Profiling may be a means of helping children to develop these skills. It allows the children to see what they have achieved and how they are progressing. The emphasis in profiling on positive statements of achievement might be more informative to children, less destructive than some types of assessment (such as formal tests) and be motivating through self-awareness and identification of areas for development. The tasks will enable you to build up a succession of formative assessments which would allow children to see progress in what they are doing.

Method

1   Select two tasks that will provide evidence for formative assessment and repeat them over time with one or more children. It would be desirable to choose one task that is highly structured and one that is more open-ended.

2   Review the tasks with the children concerned, identifying progress made and achievements arrived at. Additional material from the unit on enhancing self-esteem (Unit B2c) might also be reviewed in this context.

3   With the children decide how any evaluation sheets they have completed and the outcomes of any reviews could be used as part of a profile. Make a selection of items to be included in a child's profile.

4   If you have tried both structured and unstructured formats to elicit children's self-assessments, assess the merits of each approach.

5   Use the review questions below (taken from Wolfendale, 1987), or construct ones of your own, and complete the sheets with one or two children in your class. You can either do the sheet once only or else repeat the sheet after time has passed.

Review the sheets with the child concerned, identifying progress made and achievements arrived at. With the children, decide what use the review sheets should be put to. Make a selection of items to be included in the child's profile.

LANGUAGE

I can say my name which is.........

I know the names of parts of my body such as.........

I know the colour of my eyes which are........

I know the colour of my hair which is.............

I can put several words together, such as ....

I am still learning to pronounce some words, such as........

I can make whole sentences such as ....

I can name objects: here are some examples..........

I can ask questions, such as............

I can describe something like...............

I can answer questions, such as............

I can describe something like...................

I can point to pictures like...............

and name things in the picture, such as............

My favourite book at the moment is..............

My favourite songs and rhymes are..............

I listen to stories such as ....

Follow-up

At the end of this unit you might, on your own or with your colleagues, like to reflect on the value of self-assessment in your school.

Time needs to be given for this type of assessment to become firmly rooted in the teaching and learning environment. To a certain degree pupils need to be able to use the tools independently and, above all, the process needs to become part of ordinary classroom routine.

Not all activities lend themselves to self-assessment and used excessively it may become boring and self-defeating. It is necessary to review the matter, not only from the teacher's point of view, but also from that of the children and parents/carers.

Background information

The aim of these tasks is to investigate the degree to which self-assessment over a period of time can aid the teaching and learning process by allowing both children and teachers to see what has been achieved and what progress has been made. The secondary profiling movement has found that, on the whole, the emphasis on positive statements of achievement is more informative to children, less destructive than other forms of assessment and generally can be motivating towards the next step in self-awareness and development.

The claims for profiling have included the belief that ipsative assessment, when it is part of the formative aspects of records of achievement, is more beneficial to the individual than normative assessment. In ipsative assessment the child measures his/her current performance against his/her own past performances. In this way the assessment becomes motivational rather than judgemental. Normative assessment, on the other hand, when one's achievement is measured against the achievements of others, may promote the kind of competition where most individuals are potential losers.

Little has been tried in this field to date; so for all of us it is relatively new ground. Trial and error is the order of the day. PRAISE (DES, 1988) found that self-evaluations which were relatively unstructured gained more response from pupils but that very unstructured attempts tended to be woolly, the children being unsure as to how to go about the task. The PRAISE research was with middle and secondary pupils. It is likely that the younger the children the more need there is for a recognizable structure.

Recent research in a number of LEAs examined pupils' responses to self-evaluation in secondary schools. They found a widely differing reaction from the pupils and this was strongly related to the type of profiling they had experienced. A good many had found it very helpful but others had reservations. It seemed to suggest that it is not necessarily the process of profiling *per se* that children find helpful; the manner in which it is done is the decisive factor.

Bibliography

DES (1988) *Pilot Records of Achievement in Schools Evaluation.* London: HMSO.

Wolfendale, S. (1987) *All about Me.* London: National Children's Bureau.

Learning about Classroom Ethos from Children

Aims

To use children's evaluations of classroom ethos and classroom life to aid the teaching and learning process.

Introduction

A number of writers have produced pictures of classrooms which suggest that the experiences of the children may not be all we, as teachers, would desire for them. John Holt (1975) has maintained that children are often denied the rights of self-determination and put into situations where failure is a foregone conclusion. Jackson (1968) showed some primary children as virtual prisoners struggling between the satisfaction of personal needs and the requirements for conformity. He maintained that children have to learn to cope with three fundamental aspects of school life: learning to be alone in a crowded situation; experiencing continual evaluation; and dealing with unequal and impersonal relationships in the classroom.

Method

Choosing one of the instruments given on the following page, assess the degree to which your children think the classroom climate is a pleasant place to work in and conducive to good working relationships.

a. Clues about classroom life

So that we may get some ideas about how to make life more interesting and important for everyone in the class, each of us needs to contribute ideas about what should be improved. What things happen that shouldn't happen? What ought to happen that does not? Answer the questions below yourself and then ask the children to imagine they are a detective looking for clues to a 'good day' and a 'bad day' in this class.

What are some clues to a good day in this class? What things happen that are signs of a good day?

What are some clues to a bad day in this class? What things happen that are clues that this class is not going the way it should, or that you would like it to?

What are some things that should happen a lot more than they do to make this class a better place for learning?

b. Observing work in our class

Children in primary schools frequently work in groups. This is often a purely administrative arrangement with each pupil doing his/her individual work, but on occasion they do also work on group tasks. Using the simple observation form given below, get one or more of the children to observe the group working.

What I saw!

1. Who listened?

2. Who talked?

3. Who gave an idea?

4. I think this group was:

5. Why I think the group was that:

(taken from Schmuck and Schmuck, 1979)

Follow-up

With colleagues discuss the outcomes of the tasks and consider how the findings could inform your practice.

What evidence collected in this way might be included in your records?

Background information

Although the picture painted by some research studies appears very bleak and perhaps one that we would like to believe is at odds with our own classroom situation, there is no doubt that echoes are to be found in many classrooms. Schmuck and Schmuck (1979) have suggested ways in which teachers and children can evaluate both the classroom ethos and the degree to which the climate of the classroom is likely to promote learning or not. They highlight the importance of group processes in the classroom and suggest that most children come to school eager and well-motivated. It is up to the school and, most importantly, the class teacher to see that these propensities are developed towards good, and not debilitating, goals.

It is argued by some, Stronach (1989) for example, that a child profile *per se* is inappropriate unless the context in which it is taking place is clearly identified. The history of profiling in FE, particularly in vocational areas, has tended to place stress on self-evaluation alone without the added dimension of the social context, the resources and the political and economic demands placed on the students. Failure, however, may be related to factors other than an individual student's shortcomings. It therefore seems appropriate at this stage to attempt to gauge the degree to which the classroom influences the potential success or failure of the children.

Questions about life in classrooms and in other areas of the school have come to the fore recently with the growing disquiet about the prevalence of bullying in primary schools. Good relationships in the classroom are likely to have a knock-on effect throughout the school and making the assessment of these the background to the child's profile is essential for the successful adoption of profiling.

Brighouse (1988) has listed a series of questions schools should ask themselves in considering their children's interests. These become particularly apposite in the light of the move towards profiling.

–Does the school environment offer 'different climates' such as quiet areas and social areas? Is there access to learning at lunch times?

–What is the school's policy on bullying?

–What is the nature of any annual celebration or prize-giving?
 Are achievements in all areas given equal prominence?

–Does the school know about achievements outside school? (see Unit B8)

–What opportunities are there for mixed-age learning?

–What are the school's arrangements for ipsative competition?

–Are the school rules framed positively or negatively?

Bibliography

Brighouse, T. (1988) 'Competing with yourself can be tougher than tests', *Times Educational Supplement*, 30 September.

Hargreaves, A. (1986) 'Ideological: record breakers?', in Broadfoot, P. (ed.) *Profiles and Records of Achievement.* London: Cassell.

Holt, J. (1969) *How Children Fail.* Harmondsworth: Penguin.

Holt, J. (1975) *Escape from Childhood.* Harmondsworth: Penguin.

Jackson, P. W. (1968) *Life in Classrooms.* New York: Holt, Rinehart and Winston.

Schmuck, R. A. and Schmuck, P. A. (1979) *Group Processes in the Classroom.* Dubuque, Iowa: Wm C. Brown.

Stronach, I. (1989) 'A critique of the new assessment from currency to carnival?', in Simons, H. and Elliott, J. (eds) *Rethinking Appraisal and Assessment.* Milton Keynes: Open University Press.

Unit B5

Liaising with Others

Evaluating Contacts with Parents/Carers

Aims

To evaluate the existing contacts between parents/carers and school.

Introduction

Parents/carers have a crucial role to play in the profiling process. In early years of education the role of the parents/carers has continued to gain momentum with parents/carers coming to be seen as partners in the education process. Parents/carers are being viewed as the people who know their children best and are therefore able to present helpful information to the school and the class teacher. Parental support and participation is thus seen as being essential for profiling to the extent of regarding profiling as a dialogue between parents/carers, teachers and children.

The quality of the relationships with parents/carers, and the usefulness of parental/carers' involvement in profiling, depends on the school's approach to parents/carers and the sensitivity of individual teachers in relating to them. We begin this section by looking at the existing contacts parents/carers have with school.

Method

1   Consider the ways in which parents/carers are already involved in your school in reviewing the progress of their children and in assessment and record-keeping procedures. Compare your list with that in the *Background information* for this unit.

2   Discuss these types of involvement, addressing the following questions:

   –was the context formal or informal?

   –who initiated the contact?

   –who was asking the questions or in control?

   –who was informing whom?

   –who had 'ownership' of the situation?

   –how satisfactory is the contact likely to be for the participants?

   –what are the benefits and drawbacks of 'official' consultation meetings?

Follow-up

How could the contact you already have with parents/carers be improved for all concerned? The following units explore parent conferences as one way of improving the quality of these contacts.

Background information

Parents/carers are already likely to be involved in reviewing their children's progress in these areas:

open days/evenings for seeing work/progress;

parents'/carers' evenings for seeing the teacher individually, perhaps by appointment;

PACT-type involvement in recording reading;

meetings for parents/carers of pre-school-aged children;

interviews with teacher or headteacher requested by parent/carer;

interviews with parents/carers requested by teacher or headteacher;

'statementing' procedures;

parents'/carers' evenings or workshops with a curriculum focus;

home visits;

assemblies;

informal chats in corridors/classroom;

PTA events – sports, fetes, etc.;

work taken home by the child.

Involving Parents/Carers in Profiling

Aims

To explore the role of parents'/carers' conferences in profiling.

To provide guidance for meetings with parents/carers to discuss aspects of profiling.

To consider issues related to parents'/carers' conferences.

Introduction

This unit invites you to consider how your school should prepare for introducing parents/carers to the part they have to play in profiling and plan how you could improve the quality of meetings you have with parents. In many schools, particularly those that have adopted ILEA's Primary Language Record, parents/carers are being invited into school early in the school year to inform teachers about their child and to establish the dialogue that will continue throughout the year.

> *The purpose of the discussion between parent(s) and teacher is to encourage a two-way communication between home and school, to let parent(s) share their knowledge of the child, at home and at school, their observations and concerns, hopes and expectations.*

> (ILEA, 1988)

These conferences, with very different aims from most parent/carer interviews, have provided teachers with useful information and insights they would not otherwise have obtained and established a climate in which the parents/carers played a full part in profiling.

Method

1   Before involving the parents/carers in profiling, consider the following:

–Is there a unified school approach to profiles?

–Have the parents/carers been given any background information to introduce them to the notion of profiles and their role in developing a full picture of their child/ren? This might be through letters home, a formal parents/carers meeting or informal contacts. Before holding a meeting to introduce the parental conference in profiling, it might be worthwhile holding conferences with some supportive parents/carers beforehand and inviting them to talk at the full meeting.

–Has information for parents/carers been available in all the languages spoken in the children's homes, as well as English?

2   The first time parents/carers are involved in conferences concerning children's profiles will inevitably take longer than subsequent sessions, when the process is more familiar. Read the *Background information* about preparing for parent/carer conferences and discuss factors which will affect their success.

3   Try 'role-playing' parent conferences with a colleague, perhaps focusing on a particular child you know outside school. Try working in threes, having one person as 'teacher', one as 'parent/carer', and one as observer. Discuss how you felt as participants afterwards, and take note of the observer's comments. Observers should note aspects of body language, as well as other strategies used. After the role-play, you could try drawing up a set of guidelines for working with parents/carers.

Follow-up

Try some conferences in your school. Start with one or two parents/carers with whom you have a good relationship, and with whom you might be able to discuss the conference afterwards. Make time to share the experience with colleagues before going on to involve all the parents/carers. Discuss as a staff these trial conferences, analysing which factors affected the successful outcome of a parent/carer conference.

Background information

Preparation for a meeting with parents/carers about their involvement in profiling

Try noting the sorts of questions parents/carers might wish to ask about profiling, for example, the use of conferences to pry into the child's home life, and rehearse your responses without becoming too defensive. This can be a useful way of identifying areas of policy where you as a staff do not yet feel confident and may need more support to develop your thinking and practice.

Preparation for conferences with parents/carers

The following factors are worth considering before you try out some parent/carer conferences:

–Has enough time been allocated for each parent conference/interview? It is important to be able to chat informally to relax everyone, and to stray from the point a little if necessary to develop a good atmosphere and relationship.

–Are meetings planned for daytime (with child-care where possible) as well as in the evenings, to maximize opportunities for parents/carers to participate?

–Are translators available for parents/carers with little or no English?

–Where will the meeting take place? The setting is important to consider. If it is in the classroom, consider having some comfortable chairs (borrowed from the staffroom?) in the book corner rather than sitting at a desk, for example. Try to create a relaxing atmosphere where teacher and parents/carers can talk in confidence. Is it possible to have tea/coffee available?

—Are the parents/carers to be involved in deciding what is to be recorded? The question of who has 'ownership' of the session is important to consider, especially if parents/carers are concerned about the school 'prying' into what happens at home. Are the parents/carers free to make critical comments about the school to go on record, for example?

—What starting points for discussions could be used? Focusing on a particular piece of work, or an interest of the child's, can be useful for initiating the conference.

—Do you have a clear idea of the sorts of questions that might be asked, or areas for discussion, to help structure the session? It is important not to reduce conferences to parents/carers answering lists of questions. The talk should be open and exploratory, but some guidance can be helpful, especially in less relaxed situations. Watching TV chat show hosts can help provide pointers of what (or what not!) to do in drawing someone out in conversation.

—What techniques for encouraging parental participation in the conference can the teacher use? Using open questions, requiring more than a 'yes' or 'no' answer, nodding and making encouraging comments, and pursuing a point with an enabling question or comment (*I wonder why..., You mentioned...*), as well as offering observations based on knowledge of the child in school (*I've noticed he...*), all invite further comment.

—How will the session end? Decide on a way of winding up the session, perhaps by recapping what has been discussed, and agreeing on a summary.

Parents/carers are expecting to become more involved in their children's education, with the parents' leaflets about the National Curriculum going to all homes, and increased time allocated for meetings with parents/carers. Change in practice within schools can be very disquieting for parents/carers unless they are kept informed of what is happening and can understand the rationale and benefits of developing practice.

In recent years the government has sought to involve parents/carers more in schools through such things as the parent governor scheme and through supposed choice in selection of school. Many of these initiatives have proved to be less than satisfactory for parents/carers who, above all, seek some real involvement in their child's education. Recent moves by the DES suggest that while schools are required to provide annual reports from the summer of 1991, these can be minimal unless parents/carers request otherwise. Parents/carers can, however, if they so wish demand a more detailed profile of their child's achievement. It would therefore seem desirable on many grounds to acquire the active participation of the parents/carers in the profiling process as far as is possible.

The crucial stage to begin with parents/carers is before the child enters school, when interest is high and the information provided by the family is so advantageous to the reception class teacher. Schools already embarking on profiling, however, have found that parental support can be elicited at any point. Profiling can be utilized on open evenings as a vehicle for discussion both on progress to date and the way forward. As we saw in the section on formative assessment, parents/carers are welcoming more detailed information about the way their children are progressing. With careful introduction, the involvement of parents/carers in profiling can become the start of an improved dialogue between home and school, which can only be to the benefit of the children.

Bibliography

Hicks, J. (1986) Pupil profiling in the primary school: a review of issues, *Education Review*, 38(1).

ILEA (1988) *The Primary Language Record: Handbook for Teachers.* London: Centre for Language in Primary Education.

Teachers' Skills and Conferences with Parents/Carers

Aims

To consider the skills teachers need to run successful parent/carer conferences.

Introduction

The work done in ILEA on the Primary Language Record and its related parent conferences provided ample evidence that the success of discussions with parents/carers was dependent to a large extent on the skills of the teacher as interviewer. Headteachers are frequently engaged in one-to-one conferences with parents and may be used to discussing the most delicate matters tactfully and non-judgementally. It is important that all teachers develop such skills by reflecting on their own practice. This unit invites you to consider the skills involved and how you might improve your own capability in interviewing parents/carers.

Method

1   Read the background information and consider your own skills in the areas outlined. Identify an area that can be improved and list specific changes you could make in your approach to parent/carer interviews. Try a conference, perhaps tape-recording it (with the parents'/carers' permission). Analyse the interview and evaluate your role and the extent to which you have improved your skills.

Background information

The following have been identified as important skills for teachers in interviewing parents:

Listening skills   Allow pauses, without leaping in too quickly with another question; use 'encouragers' to signal that you are listening and to elicit further responses (saying 'Mmmm', head nodding, etc.); maintain eye contact and use welcoming, non-threatening body language.

Discussion skills   Encourage open, informal discussion, without straying too far from the point and running over time; avoid over-structuring so that it becomes a teacher-led interview; draw up a set of questions or aims that you can glance at as a reminder of important aspects; use 'open' questions, which elicit a broader response; make comments as well as asking questions, for example, 'I've noticed that in school...' and indicate by tone that parents/carers are invited to comment; allow 'verbal room' before moving on; repeat points to bring subject back to the point; summarize what has been said to return discussion to the point; set a clear 'agenda' at the beginning, making clear time constraints; decide beforehand on closing strategies (standing up, setting targets, arranging a future meeting).

Recording skills   Decide how to record the outcome (notes during the interview or at the end); ask permission to record the interview; summarize main points, agree what to record; encourage parents to sign if felt appropriate.

Some schools have found it preferable to have more parents'/carers' evenings and see fewer people each time. It is easier to form good relationships if there is not a 'production line' of parents/carers going through every ten minutes. It has also proved valuable to offer times during the day especially where child-care for younger children is available.

Liaising with Other Schools

Aims

To decide what liaison on record-keeping should be developed with other schools, including linked schools in other phases.

Introduction

One of the key aims of the National Curriculum was to make transfer from one school to another across the country easier. However, a National Curriculum on its own will not achieve that unless careful records are kept of the child's achievement and progress and appropriate liaison between institutions is achieved.

Issues of continuity are key to successful record-keeping, and so cross-phase communication is important. If the aims and nature of the profile are not discussed, the receiving school may not benefit fully from any records passed on. Equally, if feeder and receiving schools are not involved in the evaluation of the effectiveness of the records, opportunities are missed for making modifications which might improve their effect.

Method

1   As a staff, list all the possible link schools with which you already liaise or might need to liaise. These might include:

    a.   nurseries and other pre-school groups and organizations

    b.   infant schools

    c.   junior schools

d.   secondary schools

e.   local special schools and/or special needs units

f.   other non-statutory schools, such as Saturday or supplementary schools, Mosque schools, and other schools rooted in the culture and community of the children.

2   For each school:

a.   Evaluate what liaison/contact is already established. Is it adequate?

b.   How might feeder schools be involved? For example, by sharing their own records, providing dated samples of work.

c.   What is the best method of communication with schools in higher phases? For example, covering note with files sent on, meetings with first-year staff, appointing a link person for liaison, follow-up meeting to discover whether records were useful, discussing records used in that phase.

d.   Is there a need for an explanatory document to accompany profiles transferred laterally?

e.   Are any other schools in the same phase developing profiles? Is it possible to work together in clusters, learning from each other? This might also make liaison with secondary schools easier. Does the LEA have a policy on transfer documents?

f.   Do any of the children attend supplementary schools/Saturday schools or other schools connected with their language(s), culture or religion? How far is it possible and/or appropriate to involve these classes or schools in the profiling process?

3   Write up any decisions you make as part of your profiling/record-keeping policy, and provide copies for all linked schools.

Follow-up

Whatever you decide to do as a staff, it is vital that the effectiveness of such liaison is monitored. It might be that a great deal of liaison is necessary in the early stages of introducing profiles, but that, once established, less contact is necessary. Changes of staffing and revisions to the profiling process may require further liaison.

In your evaluation, try to identify which factors had an effect on the liaison process, for example, constraints of time, and how they might be overcome/reduced.

Consider other strategies for improving liaison:

a.   activities / workshops for children from different phases jointly planned by teachers from both phases;

b.   cross-phase team-teaching—for example, a reception teacher could be released to spend time working in the nursery class in the term before the children transfer;

c.   invitations to teachers from other phases to parent meetings;

d.   cross-phase INSET activities.

Background information

If we accept that profiles provide an important record of the 'whole child', and acknowledge their use in planning children's learning experiences, then it is important that the value of such records is passed on to others working with the child. However, what is passed on to schools in other phases must be in a form which is of practical use. A massive pile of dated samples reflecting the child's work throughout seven years of primary schooling may be fascinating reading, but not appropriate to pass on in that form to a secondary school. Teachers in all phases are busy people, and it may be necessary to edit a profile if it is to prove useful to other schools.

We can only find out which aspects of our records are useful by having a dialogue with receiving teachers and listening to their suggestions. Equally, the experiences of other schools in profiling can be shared and save time in development, through learning from others' experiences. Why re-invent the wheel? Cluster group meetings with feeder schools and the local secondaries could provide a useful forum for pooling profiling experiences.

Meetings held with schools and classes outside the mainstream system, such as supplementary schools, can raise awareness of the needs of children in different sectors of the community, and heighten teachers' awareness of the existence of such schools. If profiles are to reflect the whole child, then it is vital to record membership of other educational groups in the profile.

A further aspect of this is to ensure that there are full links with all the people working with a child within the school. Support teachers, community language teachers, speech therapists, etc. should all have access to, and be able to feed into, the child's profile.

Bibliography

Barrs, M., Ellis, S., Hester, H. and Thomas, A. (1990) *Patterns of Learning: The Primary Language Record and the National Curriculum.* London: Centre for Language in Primary Education.

Liaising with Governors

Aims

To explore the role of governors in relation to profiling and school record-keeping policy.

Introduction

The headteacher is employed as the principal person responsible for the internal management of the school and there are good arguments which suggest that in normal situations the head's advice should be followed in relation to these internal matters (Wragg and Partington, 1989). Nevertheless, under the 1988 Education Act the governors of a school are responsible for delivering the National Curriculum in their particular school. The school, and ultimately the governors, will be required to report to both the LEA and the DES that the National Curriculum is being fully implemented. This reporting will only be possible if adequate records have been maintained. It is in the interests of the governors, therefore, to be aware of current developments in this field.

In addition to their statutory duties, governors also perform an important role in relation to informing parents about current school developments via the annual report and reflecting parental views, and the views of the wider community which they serve, back to the school. They contribute to the promotion of the school's image in the community. It is therefore essential that they are aware of current changes both in terms of record-keeping and changes in the school's assessment policy.

In this unit you are asked to reflect on the best way of effectively communicating the essential information to governors while at the same time not overwhelming them with minutiae. There may well be resource implications from the proposed changes and these will also need to be relayed to governors.

The method used will depend on the particular relationship your school has with its governors. The way in which governors wish to discuss and use the material is likely to differ from school to school.

Method

You may choose either to write a brief report to governors or, through meetings, engage all or some of them in face to face discussions. Whichever method you choose it will be necessary to cover the following points:

a. **Background**   Governors are well aware that schools are being required to report the results of tests taken at age 11. When the results for 11-year-olds are published governors will be anxious to see that crude comparisons are not being made between individual schools. In addition they will need to be aware that testing is only one element of assessment and that the aim of the school adopting a profiling method is to encourage ipsative and formative assessment as well as summative results. The dangers of summative assessment alone need to be clearly stressed at this point.

b. **Benefits**   Governors will need to know the benefits of profiling for the children, the parents and the teachers. This section should emphasize the opportunities that profiling affords for more formative approaches to assessment, its potential for fundamentally influencing both the teaching and learning processes and its influence on the planning and delivery of the National Curriculum. The desire of both children and parents to have a final record of achievement of their primary years should also be stressed.

c. **Implementation**   Governors will then need to know what steps the school has taken in the practical implementation of profiling or in proposed developments. They will need to know about the LEA's staff development initiatives and its plans for developing profiling in a local context. At this stage examples of profiles already developed in primary schools may be appropriate.

d. **Confidentiality** Returning to record-keeping, governors will be concerned about issues relating to confidentiality of records on children. If any of your records are on computer then, under the Data Protection Act, they must be open to those reported upon. In addition the question of ownership (see Unit B3b) has been raised and this issue will also need to be communicated to governors.

In addition to formal liaison with governors, informal meetings also take place when a governor visits the school and chats to teachers. These occasions may be very fruitful for demonstrating profiling in action, its progress and limitations. Snapshots of classroom practice may provide illuminating material for governors.

If a more radical programme for informing governors is required and there is time available, profiling could become part of the governors' training programme. Governors could provide their own record of achievement similar to that prepared by course members at the beginning of the inservice period. This could include results of public examinations. Reflection on one's own life in this way often brings home the limitations of past practice and the desire to have some fuller account of one's life at school.

Bibliography

Burgess, T. and Sofer, A. (1986) *The School Governor's Handbook and Training Guide.* London: Kogan Page.

Wragg, E. C. and Partington, J. A. (1989) *A Handbook for School Governors.* London: Routledge.

Unit B6

Recording Evidence of Learning

Collecting, Selecting and Retaining Evidence of Learning

Aims

To provide experience of working collaboratively with a colleague to collect evidence of children's learning.

Introduction

The quality of teachers' judgements about children's learning is the most important factor when considering assessment. This unit invites you to collaborate with a colleague so that through a shared experience you can develop your assessment skills and consider the issues involved in collecting and using evidence of children's learning. There are many advantages to working collaboratively on an activity like this and, although it can be tackled individually, it is hoped you will be able to work with someone. This should improve the quality of the evidence of learning collected and improve the quality of decisions made regarding what the evidence tells you about the children's learning and how this might be recorded. It will involve discussion and evaluation of your work based on evidence of what happened as opposed to *impressions* of what happened.

Method

1   Plan an activity, with a colleague's help, for a group of children in a core curriculum area that will last for about an hour.

2   Implement the activity together, one observing and collecting as much evidence as possible while the other teaches, for at least 30 minutes. After a break, in which the plans for the second half can be modified if necessary, swap over roles for a further 30 minutes. The activity should include a practical

element and the learning objectives should be explicit, particularly in terms of cross-curricular skills and processes. It is desirable that the activity include an element of children's recording. You should work with a group of between four and six children but have a target child identified (the individual should not be made aware of this). The rest of the class should be working as independently as possible and both of you can assume a supervisory role. The evidence collected by the observer should include as much of the children's and teacher's utterances and behaviour as possible. This is best recorded on pages with numbered lines for ease of reference during later analysis.

3   An interview with the target child should be carried out for a few minutes at the end of the session to probe his/her achievements during the session. The questions to be asked during this should be discussed beforehand but it should be informal and other questions introduced as appropriate. A record should be kept of all the target child's contributions during this interview. Any outcomes produced by the children should be retained if possible. Immediately after the session you should both write down your impressions of the performance of each child involved (without reference to data or outcomes). Discuss your general impressions of the activity and the influence of teaching style on the evidence collected. All the evidence (including any children's outcomes) should be retained for use during a follow-up session.

Follow-up

Analyse the evidence you collected to see if your initial impressions can be supported by evidence. Modify them in the light of the evidence. This will involve fairly careful analysis since the obvious is easily overlooked!

Did the additional information you collected from the interview enable decisions about the target child to be made more readily?

Do you have any other supporting evidence of learning for the target child, in the curriculum area related to the task from previous activities, that is already recorded in some way?

What information did you gain from the children's own recording?

Examine the nature of the evidence and your decisions about the children's learning

      –in what ways are you confident about them?

      –in what ways are you less sure about them?

Which of the decisions you have made are significant enough to be worth recording and retaining in some way?

How can the child's achievements be recorded using your existing record-keeping? In what other ways could the achievements be recorded? Does your existing system need modifying?

In what ways could the decisions about a child's achievements be summarized?

Have you any evidence to support National Curriculum assessment? Are you confident that any of the evidence would allow you to say a child had achieved a particular level in a particular attainment target?

What classroom strategies would allow you to collect significant evidence of learning similar to any collected during the collaborative work with your colleague?

What are the advantages and disadvantages of working collaboratively in this way?

To what extent has this activity addressed the four steps outlined in the background information (and Unit A5)?

To what extent do you now consider your recording system to be 'fit for the purpose' of allowing you to challenge, if ever necessary, SAT results (see Unit A2)?

Background information

Children produce a whole range of evidence as they engage in classroom activities. This evidence has to be interpreted by the teacher to help her understand what the child knows, understands and can do. This activity is intended to enhance your skills in active listening and responsive questioning so that you will be better able to gain insight into children's learning and record the judgements you make. The situation where two adults work with one group of children is obviously impractical in most classroom situations. However, it is hoped that the experience will help 'sharpen' the judgements you make in the normal classroom context. The extensive data produced during the activity are not intended to represent the practice in the usual classroom where the raw data would be much less.

In the context of this unit it is worth restating the steps involved in collecting and recording evidence of learning described in Unit A5.

Step 1 – the raw evidence (teachers' notes, children's recording, tapes, etc.)

Step 2 – judgements supported by evidence selected from the raw data.

Step 3 – records which amount to a summary of evidence of the judgements made at step 2.

Step 4 – summative report (as required by the DES).

The activity should have helped you appreciate the difficulties involved in moving from step 2 to step 3 and the dangers of ticking boxes without supporting evidence for the implicit judgements.

Using Children's Recording

Aims

To evaluate which examples of children's outcomes provide the most useful evidence of learning.

To explore ways in which children can record their own achievements.

Introduction

'Children's recording' has two distinct meanings in this unit. The first part looks at the variety of recording children engage in as part of the learning process, that is the outcomes of their work, and how these outcomes can be used to provide evidence of learning. Teachers often use children's work as the main way of assessing progress. However, children's outcomes can often mislead us in terms of the learning that has been involved. The tasks below are intended to help you look critically at the nature of the insight we can gain from certain kinds of outcome and appreciate the need to collect other kinds of evidence to support judgements made about children's work.

The second part examines ways in which children can record their own achievements. Children are becoming increasingly involved in recording their own learning, both incidentally and in more formal settings. Children's records may include the list of books being read, chosen dated samples in a folder, or formal workwheels or worksheets of completed tasks. As teachers (and children) develop their methodology in record-keeping, it is important to evaluate the usefulness of these types of record.

Part 1 – Outcomes of children's work

Method

1   List all the ways in which children have produced outcomes during the last week that could be used as evidence of learning.

2   Collect a sample of these and, with a colleague, analyse what insight can be gained into the child's learning from the outcome or recording.

> Are some types of children's recording more useful in this respect than others?

> Which provide insight into the children's ideas or explanations?

> What else did you need to know to make judgements about the work?

> What are the advantages and disadvantages of using children's work as evidence of learning?

3   What is the most efficient way of recording your judgements about the children's outcomes?

Follow-up

Look at the examples listed in the *Background information.*

Try out some of the ideas which you do not usually use with children in your class.

How can you encourage children to record their work in a way that makes it more suited to assessment?

Discuss what you have tried with colleagues and share your ideas.

Background information

The outcomes children produce as a part of a learning experience might include:

picture with teacher's caption;

picture with dictated caption;

picture with written caption;

written work;

models;

computer data-files (for example, Writer or Our Facts);

graphs, tables or diagrams;

audio or video tape;

work-sheets;

questionnaires;

concept maps.

Each of these can provide evidence of learning, but that evidence is likely to be more useful if it includes something about the process as well as the product. It is also important to include with the outcome, if it is to be retained (see Unit B6c), some indication of the learning context (see Unit B6d).

Part 2 – Children recording their own achievements

Method

1   If the children in your school are not involved, at present, in recording their own activities, achievements or progress:

a.   List the ways in which children could be recording their own achievements. Include items such as records of books read, activities covered, and evaluation reports of practical tasks such as design and technology.

b.   Consider the formats that would make them suitable for use in your class.

c.   Discuss with your children what sorts of records they might keep. It would probably be best to focus on one or two areas only, possibly:

–a reading record

–a record of tasks completed through the week

–a maths record

–a record of work completed as part of the topic

d.   Choose one of the records to try out in your class before proceeding with the rest of the tasks.

e.   Try discussing with teachers from other schools what forms of children's records they use, and collect examples of possible records.

2   If you already get children to record their achievements, collect examples in a range of curriculum contexts and formats. Discuss with the children how useful they find each form of record in reviewing their progress.

3   In groups, share your examples of children's records and sort them into their various types.

a.　What are the aims of each type of record? Whom are they meant to inform and about what?

b.　Which forms of recording are most informative for you as teachers?

c.　Which records did the children find most helpful?

d.　Which factors about each record seem to affect their usefulness?

　　–the format?

　　–the curriculum area?

　　–time given for completion?

　　–frequency of use?

　　–whether the child was involved in devising the record?

4　Draw up a list of factors which influence the effectiveness of children's records.

Follow-up

Try out your chosen form(s) of child's records for half a term, and then review. Include the children in the review process and amend or reject any forms of record which are not felt to be of practical use.

Background information

Involving children in recording their own learning encourages a feeling of ownership of, and involvement in, the learning process. It also encourages greater autonomy in working in the classroom. Children can see their work in terms of blocks of time with set tasks and can move through a range of activities without having to ask the teacher 'What can I do now?'. This frees the teacher for working with particular groups or individuals and is an important factor in classroom organization for effective teaching and learning.

In reading, children's own records can help them to review their progress and develop a critical awareness of their patterns of reading. Are they reading frequently enough, fast enough and from a range of authors/genres?

In writing, the work of Donald Graves has suggested ways of involving children in recording the range and scope of their writing, and this has helped children to set themselves goals in the development of their writing in both composition and transcription elements (English ATs 3 and 5). In oracy, some teachers have been involving children in evaluating their contributions to discussions and offering them feedback. The work of the National Oracy Project is further developing this. In creative arts children can develop portfolios of their work to exemplify their developing skills across the year. In Design and Technology, 'evaluation' is one of the attainment targets and encouraging children to record their work in that area is particularly relevant. With an area like IT, where limited resources are available and careful management of the resource is essential, the child's record can be a valuable tool for classroom management. The need for teachers to record the experiences a child has had in order to provide evidence that the children have covered statutory programmes of study can be met through this type of child's record.

One effect of children's self-evaluation through record-keeping is a development of self-discipline. If, when reviewing a child's records, s/he is involved in discussing why a particular activity/task was successful (or not), then aspects of the child's behaviour will often arise, and possible solutions will be discussed. For example, it may be that one task took a long time because the child was working with or near a particular friend, and will admit to becoming excited and easily distracted when working with that child. An agreement can then be reached to ensure that s/he mixes with that friend for practical activities, or play times, but not when working on tasks requiring greater concentration and application. It can help the child to make the connection between behaviour and learning, and make a viable 'learning contract' with the teacher. The links with self-assessment are obvious and teachers should refer to Unit B4 to develop this theme further.

Bibliography

Graves, D. (1983) *Writing: Teachers and Children at Work.* London: Heinemann.

Watt, D. (1990) 'Evidence of learning', *Child Education*, January.

Selecting Children's Work for the Profile

Aims

To help teachers to discuss and decide on a school policy for selecting and storing children's work as evidence of their learning

Introduction

Schools have always kept a proportion of children's work for a period of time as evidence of learning. Such samples have often played an important part in parents'/carers' evenings. The practice of keeping systematic examples of children's work showing development over a period was recommended by HMI in the 1978 Primary Survey (DES, 1988). Now such material should be kept systematically to give a usable source of evidence about children's learning for National Curriculum assessments and should become a part of the child's profile. This unit is concerned with how to go about this and how selections of children's work should be made.

Method

1   Make a selection of five examples of children's work to bring to a staff meeting. Discuss the reasons you chose particular pieces.

2   As a whole staff, examine the following questions and draw up a draft policy for the selection of children's work:

What range of work will be selected?

What purposes will the selection serve?

Should the work be annotated by the teacher? (Unit B6d addresses this in more detail.)

Who should see it?

Is the material to be available to be seen by the child and the parents/carers?

Where does it finish up?

Does the child take it home?

Who will have ownership of it at the end?

Follow-up

After a period of collecting, annotating and storing examples of children's work, review as a staff the purposes of the material kept, the practical problems involved and the usefulness of the material for informing future planning.

After a parents'/carers' evening, review the value of the selected work in providing parents/carers with a useful picture of their child's achievements.

Reconsider your policy on the selection and storage of children's work.

Do you now have a manageable policy?

List the areas of policy on which you agreed.

List the areas on which you disagreed.

List the actions which need to be taken to put the policy into practice.

Background information

John MacGregor, when he was the Secretary of State for Education, announced at the AMMA Conference (Easter 1990) that teachers should not feel under pressure to hoard large amounts of evidence to support their assessments.'Recording must support assessment, not become a substitute for it. Teachers must be free to develop whatever approach to recording suits their own teaching style.' (Blackburn, 1990)

This was one of the then Secretary of State's moves to try to alleviate pressure on teachers in the wake of the 1988 Education Reform Act. However, it was timely in that it did reinforce the idea of making sensible judgements about what evidence to collect of children's learning instead of trying to hang on to everything.

Sampling in assessment

Selection, or sampling, is an important factor in assessment. Any assessment process must involve choosing some items to assess and not others. When we take a driving test we are only assessed on certain examples of driving behaviour: driving in traffic, three-point turn, turning right at traffic lights, etc. We are not assessed on driving on a motorway in fog or parking in a supermarket car park on Saturday morning.

The important thing is that the choice of items gives the evidence of the child's learning. The driving test is intended to give evidence that the driver can cope reasonably well with any normal driving situation. So, if you can do a three-point turn, you should have a fair chance in the supermarket's car park. The trouble with the driving test and similar forms of assessment is that you have to take it on a particular day when you might not be feeling well or you might be very nervous and not be able to give the evidence which is required. Teacher assessment is fortunately not like this. We can choose which items we will use as evidence of learning; we can choose when to collect the evidence: we don't have to take evidence at a particular date or time. We do have control over the way the sample is taken in the way that a standardized test does not.

We need to decide, though, on what basis we are sampling and what criteria we are using for the sampling. Children's learning behaviour is one source of evidence. Another major source of evidence is the work which children produce during the course of their learning: pictures, writing, models, etc. In this unit we are looking particularly at selecting items of work that children have produced and making decisions about how many and which items to store. It is obviously better not to keep everything. Much more is to be gained from keeping a small sample which has been carefully selected and documented.

Criteria for sampling

A selection of the child's work can serve two purposes:

1   to give a picture of the quality range of work which has been produced over a period of time;

2   to give evidence of achievement.

In choosing the work for the collection we can take three possible approaches:

1   a random sample;

2   a structured sample of good, middling and poor;

3   only the best of the work.

A random sample of work can be taken by selecting a day in the term when everything which the child does is collected and stored. Alternatively, front, middle and end pages of books can be removed and retained.

One of the points about profiling is that it should reflect the child's achievements, rather than failures. It was suggested by the *RANSC Report* (DES, 1989) that only the child's best work be retained.

Another factor to take into consideration is the range of curriculum coverage and the relationship to National Curriculum Attainment Targets. It is possible to establish a list of Attainment Targets for which evidence of attainment is sought through the child's work.

The timing of selection is important. If this is done on a fixed date then it limits the kind of selection which can be made. An ongoing selection of appropriate material is consistent with a formative approach to assessment.

Who makes the selection?

Profiling includes the idea that the child should have some involvement in what goes into the profile and have a sense of ownership of it. This applies also to the selection of children's work. Children's sharing in the selection process helps to give this sense of involvement, pride in the collection of work and, thus, can contribute significantly to the child's motivation and enthusiasm for school. It also helps to bridge the gap between home and school where the child can feel that the school is responsive to his/her priorities.

This can be achieved by allowing children to select a number of pieces of work, say each half term, which are to be kept, or by allowing children to nominate work to be kept as they do it. There is some evidence from secondary schools that where pupils are allowed to make their own selection of work, or contributions to a written profile, they feel ownership of the record and are increasingly motivated towards school (DES, 1989).

This also brings up again the question of the type of work selected. If we decide to keep only the best of the child's work, who decides which is the best? Do we allow children to be involved in that decision? Do children know which is their best work?

We may not wish to surrender the decision about the selection entirely to the child, yet still want the child's involvement. It is possible to suggest a negotiated decision between the teacher and the child in consultation. This would be consistent with current developments in negotiated learning and children's involvement in planning and evaluation.

A further point about selection is that it might be possible for work done at home to be included. This, again, strengthens the bond between home and school and increases the parents'/carers' and the child's sense of involvement with the school.

Who should see the selected work?

Whereas in the past schools have made samples of children's current work available for parents/carers to see, especially on parents'/carers' evenings, we have not usually kept a developmental set of materials for parents/carers and the child to be able to look through at any time. If the collection of material is to be available to be seen by the child and the parents/carers, this will involve storage or presentation in an easily accessible form.

Who owns the final portfolio of work?

There are a number of questions here: What happens to the selected work at the end? Will the parent/carer or the child be able to take the collection of work away? When is the end? Should the collection be sent on to the secondary school? If the child is involved in the selection, the sense of ownership is bound to be increased and the motivation to be allowed to keep the material is bound to be stronger. It is likely that parents/carers would value a collection of their child's work which has been catalogued and labelled. The use of photographs of the child in school situations could also play a significant part in this and would help to increase the motivational effects.

How long we keep the material also needs to be considered. If we are to allow it to be taken by the parents/carers and child, then they will be interested in having it at an early stage. It may be sensible, therefore, to release the collection at the end of each year, or at the end of each key stage.

How is the work to be documented and stored?

As a record of the child's progress, there is little to be gained by simply keeping items in a folder. It is possible to label items with

Date

Context

Whether the work is a first or final draft

Evidence of learning

Comment on the child's achievement in relation to previous work

There is more about some of these aspects in Unit B6d.

It is necessary to identify the type of material which can be stored and to make provision for this. Large art folders are necessary to store pictures.

Photographs of models can be used very effectively. Taking the photographs increases the child's motivation and sense of importance.

As mentioned earlier, photographs of children taking part in activities in the classroom can also form part of the record. This has a highly motivating effect. It makes the child more reflective about what s/he is doing (see Unit B2c).

The storing of collaborative work can be a problem where more than one child is responsible for the outcome. In this case it is better to store it for one child and indicate the child's contribution in the note.

Bibliography

Blackburn, L. (1990) 'Government relents on SATs proposal', *Times Educational Supplement,* 13 April, p. 5.

DES (1978) *Primary Education in England.* London: HMSO.

DES (1989) *Records of Achievement National Steering Committee Report.* London: HMSO.

Recording Information about Context

Aims

To investigate what information about the context of children's work needs recording.

Introduction

When assessing children's work, both in process and product, it is important that the context and its effects on the child are considered. By recording aspects of context, it may be possible to assess how the child performs in various contexts, and to plan for more effective learning experiences.

Method

1   Choose a child on whom to focus. Observe the child working in two different curriculum contexts, one practical task and one involving a written outcome. Collect samples of any work produced, and make notes on the social and curriculum context in which the child was working. You might consider the following questions:

    a.   Was the work initiated by the teacher or the child?

    b.   Was the child working alone or with others?

    c.   If in a group, how was it composed, for example, friendship, attainment?

    d.   Where was the child working?
          At a group table in the centre of the room, in a quiet bay, sitting on the carpet?

    e.   How much teacher/child interaction was there? Who initiated any interactions and what was their nature?

    f.   What curriculum areas did the work involve?

    h.   Who decided when the task was completed? How?

i.   What was the child's attitude to the task, both during the process, and in response to any product?

j.   Did the child perform differently on the two tasks? What factors affected this?

2   Discuss each child's work, and how far the contexts affected the learning. What implications are there for the teacher's further planning in each case? Draw up a list of factors relating to context which might be important to record when assessing children's work. Discuss changes which might need to be developed in teaching styles, organization and planning to take full account of the effects of context on children's work.

Follow-up

Use the list produced to record important contextual factors relating to notes in children's records and samples of written work, etc.

It might be helpful to draw up a pro forma or matrix for recording aspects of context to reduce the workload.

Review after half a term and revise the list if necessary.

Background information

The recording of aspects of context pertinent to children's writing was formalized in the ILEA Primary Language Record and was found to have a beneficial effect on the teacher's perceptions and understanding of the child's learning. The effect of the curriculum context has been highlighted for some years (DES, 1975; Barnes, Britton and Rosen, 1969). But it is through the emphasis on real purposes for writing, exemplified by the projects and publications of the National Writing Project, that context has come to the fore. By noting the contexts for learning, whether in writing or any other activity, teachers can have greater insight into the child's learning, and plan their subsequent teaching strategies.

Where work has been initiated by children, and where the children have a clear understanding of the learning aims for an activity (see Unit B4a), their motivation is often greater than where they are engaged in teacher-directed tasks with no clear aims.

When children work collaboratively there can be benefits in terms of learning, but the groups need careful monitoring since children will work better in some groupings than others, and it is important for the teacher to note the effect of the group on the individual's performance. It may be necessary in future planning to try different groups in terms of ability, age, gender, friendship or personality.

The physical context can have a profound effect too. Some teachers have found it necessary to rearrange their classrooms to provide quiet working spaces where children can work alone or in pairs without disturbance, as well as having group tables and spaces for collaborative work. The traditional classroom with all the storage round the edges of the room and the tables in the middle may not meet the needs of the children.

Children may perform differently in particular curriculum areas – a child who is judged as having writing difficulties because s/he only produces three lines of a story may be able to write pages about a science activity, or be able to sit engrossed for long periods when working with figures. This has implications for the grouping of children according to attainment. Children are often placed in 'ability' groups having been judged on one criterion – reading ability or the stage of maths they are at – and these groups can remain for work across the whole curriculum. Monitoring performance in different curriculum contexts can challenge this.

Bibliography

Barrs, M., Ellis, S., Hester, H. and Thomas, A. (1990) *Patterns of Learning: The Primary Language Record and the National Curriculum.* London: Centre for Language in Primary Education.

Barnes, G., Britton, J. and Rosen, H. (1969) *Language, the Learner and the School.* Harmondsworth: Penguin.

DES (1975) *A Language for Life* (Bullock Report). London: HMSO.

ILEA (1988) *Primary Language Record: Handbook for Teachers.* London: Centre for Language in Primary Education.

Unit B7

Recording Personal Qualities

Aims

To consider the value of and concerns about the assessment of personal qualities as part of a child's profile.

Introduction

Profiling has often included an element that relates to the personal characteristics of the pupil being profiled. The *RANSC Report* (DES, 1989) recommended that qualities such as reliability and enthusiasm should be included in a record of achievement. The justification for this is based on the fact that many commendable virtues such as perseverance, tenacity, the ability to work co-operatively with others etc. have not formed a substantial part of assessment and more easily assessable skills have been likely to take precedence. In producing a more rounded picture of the child, it is argued, the profile will fill the gaps that conventional assessment has omitted. In this context the lack of personal and social education as part of the National Curriculum is also significant.

However, this area of profiling is fraught with difficulties. If the teacher is to do the assessment there inevitably arise questions of validity. Psychologists have questioned whether teachers have sufficient knowledge to be able to assess personality. In addition, as we have seen from Unit B2b it is not easy to make personal assessments without allowing bias to enter in the form of gender, race or class. Furthermore, most comments about personal qualities suggest that these are personal traits in the psychometric tradition; no account is taken of the circumstances under which these qualities might be displayed.

Method

1   As a staff, select two pupils with whom you are all acquainted and write brief portraits of these pupils emphasizing their personal characteristics. If it is appropriate two of the children chosen from Unit B2b could be utilized.

The pen-portraits should then be compared verbally and the language examined in ways outlined in Unit B2b. Any agreements or disagreements should be explored in more detail.

2   Consider whether the assessments of personality are based on concrete and demonstrable evidence, or whether they are more in the form of 'gut' feelings.

It is important to consider next how the personality comments can be generalized to situations outside the classroom or outside the school and to investigate the degree to which your assessment of a child's personality is supported by the child him/herself.

3   List a set of descriptors that you commonly use to describe children and write these words out individually on cards.

Working with individual children, sort the cards into three piles: Like me – unlike me – unsure.

Compare the child's own assessment with the one you have made.

With younger children it will be necessary to select the vocabulary carefully in order for it both to be intelligible and to allow you to do the task. You could use pictures involving facial expressions instead of words.

Follow-up

Read the *Background information* and discuss some of the issues raised. Consider the implications for classroom practice and school policy.

Background information

As we have previously noticed, evidence suggests that children acquire a 'staffroom personality'. Thus staff may talk about individual children in the staffroom on numerous occasions and a group labelling of a particular child may emerge. This may be a positive image resulting in a halo effect – a situation where an individual is seen as 'a good pupil' in certain circumstances. This belief is extended to include every circumstance, although careful investigation of the evidence might suggest that this is not so. Conversely it may result in a uniformly negative perspective.

It is important to review the background against which teachers' comments are made. Some famous individuals, Churchill and Einstein, to name but two, had far from satisfactory school reports. This might suggest that favourable characteristics in school are not necessarily predictive of behaviour in other contexts.

Some writers, Stronach (1989) for example, have questioned the purpose and validity of profiles in general and the assessment of personal characteristics in particular. In tracing the historical roots of profiling he suggests that what started as a concern for self-development and vocational training in the 1960s developed in subsequent decades into a tool for servicing employers' needs. The needs of the employers and the needs of the workers may be at odds. Employers often see improvements in self-concept in terms of producing better worker attitudes for example but employees might look to greater variety of work as a more concrete gain.

The question returns again to what are considered *desirable* personal characteristics and the degree to which these traits are rooted in the particular needs of the time. In past decades the needs of the individual as far as education is concerned and his/her rights to self-determination have been a central issue in primary education. In recent years, and since the 1988 Education Reform Act, there has been a strong desire to favour the world of work and the needs of society as a whole over the desire for individual growth. The ideal pupil in this era may therefore be adaptable, hard-working, responsible and self-reliant. Desirable qualities no doubt. But a different era might stress other qualities like the ability to co-operate with others, being creative or less malleable. It is important then in looking at personal characteristics to think clearly why we consider certain attributes to be desirable, what model of the child these are seeking to describe and whether they are intended for the child's own self-development or to serve the needs of others.

Stronach maintains that the profile is geared towards a particular view of the self and not towards the learning process. It becomes in this sense a tool for surveillance and controlling individuals: pupil-focused but not pupil-centred. He goes on to argue that it is the opposite to child-centredness as Rousseau and others in the progressive tradition visualized it:

> *At the heart of the pupil centredness of profiling and reviewing lies an educational paradox: by constructing the student-centred, holistic and personalised profile, we de-individualise the learners by asking each of them at the same time to conform to a stereotype and to be themselves. In that sense perhaps there is no alienation more subtle than self assessment.*

(Stronach, 1989, p.170)

You may consider the views stated above to be extreme. In some form or another, however, the uneasiness raised by personal aspects of profiles has troubled a number of writers. By moving into profiling primary teachers will be in a position to gather far more information about children than has been possible to date. Do you think this is a desirable move or are there some areas of a child's life that should remain away from public scrutiny? Are we in danger of becoming the all-seeing and all-knowing professionals that some teachers portray to children, and is this an intrusion into personal liberty?

Bibliography

DES (1989) *Records of Achievement National Steering Commitee Report,* London: HMSO.

Stronach, I. (1989) 'A critique of the new assessment from currency to carnival?', in Simons, H. and Elliott, J. (eds) *Rethinking Appraisal and Assessment.* Milton Keynes: Open University Press.

Methods to Assess and Record Personal Qualities

Aims

To evaluate methods which could be used in the assessment and recording of personal qualities as part of a child's profile.

Introduction

In Unit B7a, we considered whether profiles should involve a record of personal qualities and the difficulties that such a record entailed. We also questioned whether personal qualities are meaningful when they are recorded out of context and whether behaviour in school necessarily mirrors behaviour at home or in other social contexts. Profiling at secondary and FE level has frequently included some assessment of personal characteristics. Very often these take the form of simple check lists in which pupils can check off those characteristics which most seem to describe themselves. At other times they might include a written portrait of 'myself'.

In Unit B7b we have composed portraits of children from the knowledge that we as teachers have of the children we come into contact with on a daily basis. In the case of young children, however, it has long been suggested that parents/carers are in a better position to report and record their own children's behaviour and that winning the confidence and co-operation of the parents/carers might be an important element in making a profile a success. In addition, the profiling movement has highlighted the importance of personal assessment and therefore it is crucial not to overlook the children themselves as important contributors to this kind of assessment.

Method

1   Choose one or two older children and ask them to write a brief portrait of themselves. If either of these children was chosen for task B7a then you could compare their portrait with the one you compiled. If they differ you will need to decide how this contradiction can be resolved for the profile.

Profiling with older children has often provided a list of characteristics which the children check off as appropriate. Devise a list of characteristics that you would find suitable and allow the children to tick those which apply to them. Once again care will be needed with language to make sure that it is appropriate to the children's age.

2   With younger children it might be much simpler and more advantageous for all concerned if parents/carers and children together completed a task on personal evaluation. Below are three tasks taken from Wolfendale (1989). They are intended for use with children who are about to enter full-time education for the first time, but are appropriate with adaptation for any children at Key Stage 1.

Choose one task for parents/carers and children to try together. This task will need some introduction to parents/carers prior to the children taking the form home.

1.   My moods and feelings

Now

I am happy when ....

I look forward to ....

I cry when ....

I get upset when ....

I am naughty when ....

I get cross when ....

I get worried when ....

I am frightened by ....

I don't like ....

I get sad when ....

Best of all I like ....

What makes me excited is ....

I AM OLD ENOUGH NOW TO DESCRIBE MY FEELINGS:
YES / NO

What else is there to say about me ....

....

2. Beginnings

Some things we might remember are:

When I first smiled ....laughed ....

What made me cry ....

What made me upset ....

What I liked doing in my pram, or cot............

Who I liked to be cuddled by ....

3. Now

I have ....sister(s) aged ....

I have ....brother(s) aged ....

Other people I live with are ....

I like playing with ....

I enjoy being with ....especially when ....

....

I look forward to seeing ....

I get on best with ....

I love..

I don't like ....

I co-operate when ....

When I am told off I ....

When I am praised I ....

I help at home YES / NO and my favourite job is ....

My favourite time of day is ....

Follow-up

Review your views as a staff about the value, difficulties and issues related to assessing personal qualities. What kind of record is most suitable for recording personal qualities if you choose to include them in a profile? Consider the advantages of producing an Entry Profile for children when they enter your school. How might such evidence of base line achievements be used alongside a school's results in terms of the children's National Curriculum achievements?

Bibliography

Wolfendale, S. (1989) *All about Me.* London: National Children's Bureau.

Unit B8

Knowledge of Children Outside the Classroom

Aims

To help teachers to consider their awareness of children's interests, knowledge, achievement and relationships outside the school and the relevance of this to profiling.

Introduction

It is likely that we tend to know relatively little about our children's out-of-school lives. We often ask children to talk and write about themselves. But what do we learn from this? Often what we are told does not give us evidence of their achievements out of school. The first thing we need to be able to do is to help children to share with us their experiences and their achievements. Such sharing is intended to make the child feel a continuity between her life at home and school and help her to understand better the function of the curriculum at school and its relationship to home life.

The first step in this is to consider how much we already know about children outside the school.

Method

1   Choose three children whom you would consider strong, average and weak academically (use different children from those used in Unit B2). Write down anything you know about their lives out of school.

2   Examine your list of facts.

      What do you find that you do not know?

      Make a list of these.

The following are some suggested areas.

The child's social experiences and the effect of these upon the child's life at home and in school:

    a.   Role of a grandparent in the child's learning.

    b.   The role of childminders in the child's learning.

    c.   The child's relationship with parents/carers and their view of the child as a learner.

Learning behaviour outside school:

    a.   Does the child engage in reading, writing, creative activities in the home?

    b.   What happens with the child's peers in the playground and at home?

    c.   How much time does the child spend watching the television and what is learned from this?

Follow-up

What strategies would enable you to elicit information from children about their lives outside of the classroom?

Background information

Why should we want to record information about the child out of school?

Profiling is concerned with recording the child's achievements. While we have children at school for a good proportion of their lives, they spend a great deal of time in other contexts, with peer groups, parents, other relatives and other adults. It can be argued that these other contexts are possible sources of achievement. To know more about children's out-of-school lives and activities will help give us a broader view of the child.

The Records of Achievement movement in secondary schools has found that pupils benefit from being able to record their out-of-school achievements (see the *RANSC Report,* DES, 1989). The increased motivation which is given to secondary pupils through this might be reflected in primary children. Primary schools have always looked towards good home relationships, and a smooth transition between home and school is an aim which most primary schools would share for Key Stage 1.

Wells (1987) and Tizard and Hughes (1984) are among a number of researchers who show that the experiences which children have in the home are often very positive ones. They are critical of the experiences which many children have when they attend school in a 1-in-30 context with highly structured and limited interactions with adults. They point out that often the child is engaged in a more sympathetic interaction with adults in the home than in the classroom. Wells shows this to be true regardless of social class.

For some children the link between home and school is not an easy one. John Holt (1969) refers to the 'lack of reality' which some children sense in school because it is so remote from the culture of the home. It is widely demonstrated that children's background experiences affect their learning in school. There may be factors in the home and peer environment which are blocking their learning at school. But how much do we find out about this?

It is very easy for us as teachers to develop stereotyped images about children's home backgrounds and to make assumptions about the kind of experiences they have in the home based, for example, upon the way they are dressed or the way in which they speak (see Unit B2 on Images of Children). But how much do we really know? The following unit will explore strategies to help you extend your knowledge of children outside the class.

Bibliography

DES (1989)   *Records of Achievement National Steering Committee Report.* London: HMSO.

Holt, J. (1969) *How Children Fail.* Harmondsworth: Penguin.

Tizard, B. and Hughes, M. (1984) *Young Children Learning.* London: Fontana.

Wells, C. G. (1987) *The Meaning Makers.* London: Heinemann.

Conferencing with Children about Life out of School

Aims

To introduce the idea of conferencing with children for the purposes of profiling and to consider some of the techniques in talking with individual children.

Introduction

Conferencing is not new: it means talking with children and it is fatuous to suppose that teachers need to learn how to do this! However, it will be noted here that many interactions we have with children in the 'normal' classroom teaching situation are different from those involved in the conferencing mode. In conferencing, the objective is to get an open and honest account from the child and to encourage the child to take the initiative in thinking. If profiles are to give a more rounded picture of the child, we need to encourage this kind of open dialogue in order to get accurate and honest information from the child about home background, perceptions of the learning situation in the classroom and any relevant features of the child's life.

Method

1   Devise questions, or a questionnaire, for a conference with a child about out-of-school activity.

In doing this try to convey the impression that:

   a.   any information is allowed

   b.   you are interested in particular and general instances: 'once I ... ', or 'I always ... '

   c.   you would like the child to evaluate her experiences and achievements in terms of which ones are important or significant

2   Go back to the list of points which you made in Unit B8a to decide what areas you think you might need to know about.

The following are some suggestions:

What I like to do best at home is ....

The most important things I do at home are ....

What I hate doing at home is ....

The most interesting thing I have done at home is ....

The person who helps me with things the most is ....

Follow-up

What information do you anticipate learning from conferencing that is not easy to obtain in other ways?

Background information

Format for the conference   There are various possibilities, depending on the child. It is a matter of how to present the 'questions' to the child in a way which leaves the child able to take initiatives and to respond openly. A way to do this is not to 'ask questions', but to offer suggestions for dialogue: 'What I like about … is… '. This takes the child out of the format of responding to the teacher's direct questions and can allow the child to think more openly. This method will be further discussed in Unit B8c, when you will be asked to carry out a conference on home background.

Teachers' questions   Asking children questions is part of the bread and butter of the teaching and learning process. But we need to reflect on the ways in which we ask questions and the purposes of questions. There is some interesting research on teachers' interactions with children in classrooms. ORACLE, for example (Galton, Simon and Croll, 1980), shows that individual teachers' interactions with children tend to be of a rather 'low-level' kind, concerning basic organizational matters and classroom housekeeping. It is with the class that the teacher tends to ask more demanding questions and to get children thinking in depth.

The use of 'open' and 'closed' questions is now a well-known feature of classroom teaching. Here the teacher asks questions which encourage a closed 'knowledge' of the answer:

Teacher: How do rabbits protect themselves from their enemies?

Child: By running fast.

Teacher: Good. Any other ways?

Child: By making holes in the ground.

Teacher: Yes.

                What do we call it when rabbits dig down into the ground?

Child: Burrowing.

Teacher: Burrowing, that's right.

                Does anybody know the name for the burrow where lots of rabbits live?

Child: A warren.

Teacher: Good.

It is also worth noting that these are 'pseudo questions': questions posed in order to make teaching points and to help children to think, not in order to gain information.

This 'questioning as teaching' tends to involve the use of closed questions as the teacher uses it to elicit the responses which she needs in order to make the specific teaching points she is aiming at (for example, how rabbits protect themselves). Willes (1983) shows how children learn, in the early years of school, what the rules of this game are. Holt (1969) calls it the 'read my mind game', meaning that children work out that the teacher is looking for a particular response and the winner is the one who can give it to her.

Jane French (1987) shows how the questions which teachers ask fall into a three-part structure:

1. **Initiation**

2. **Response**

3. **Feedback**

This can often be the format even in conversation with an individual child:

Teacher:	(1)	Have you got any pets?
Child:	(2)	Yes, a rabbit.
Teacher:	(3)	That's nice.
	(1)	What's his name?
Child:	(2)	Peter.
Teacher:	(3)	Mm.
	(1)	Do you keep him inside the house, or outside?
Child:	(2)	Outside.
Teacher:	(3/1)	Doesn't he get cold in the winter?

The problem for us is that, once children learn that this is the way to respond to teachers' questions, it can block a more open response to attempts to gain information and prevent the child from taking the initiative in the dialogue.

How then do we manage to elicit the kind of information about children's out-of-school situation which we need? It will mean asking questions of a different kind and in a different way.

Conferencing has been introduced in the National Writing Project and is described in some detail for the discussion of children's drafting and redrafting in Graves (1983, Chapter 2). This is worth looking at to show the ways in which Graves sees children taking the initiative in devising subjects for their writing.

The point is that we should convey to children that any possibilities are acceptable in the first instance. The child is able to 'brainstorm' ideas and rule out those which she thinks will not work.

A similar approach is needed here so that the child does not imagine that we are looking for a certain category of information (reading the teacher's mind). However, we do need some kind of prompt. An open task in which the child is asked to initiate ideas about him/herself is therefore required.

Key aspects of the conference, then, are:

> the relationship with the child should be relaxed and open;
>
> the child should not feel threatened;
>
> the child should feel that it is all right to say anything;
>
> the child should feel able to take the initiative;
>
> the child should be able to take the task seriously and feel that she is being heard sympathetically.

Bibliography

French, J. (1987) 'Language in the Primary Classroom', in Delamont, S. *The Primary School Teacher.* Lewes: Falmer Press.

Galton, M., Simon, B., and Croll, P. (1980) *Inside the Primary Classroom.* London: Routledge and Kegan Paul.

Graves, D. (1983) *Teachers and Children at Work.* London: Heinemann.

Holt, J. (1969) *How Children Fail.* Harmondsworth: Penguin.

Tizard, B. *et al.* (1988) *Young Children at School in the Inner City.* London: Lawrence Erlbaum Associates.

Wells, C. G. (1986) *The Meaning Makers.* London: Heinemann.

Willes, M. (1983) *Children into Pupils.* London: Routledge and Kegan Paul.

Carrying out a Conference with the Child on Home Background

Aim

To carry out a conference with a child about aspects of his/her home background.

Introduction

Now that you have considered some of the techniques of conferencing with children, noted your own knowledge about the children's backgrounds and devised a format for conducting the conference, it is time to carry out the conference with the child.

This task is intended to bring out any significant aspects of the home background, although specific aspects to be followed up later may occur.

Method

1   Use the questions or questionnaire (produced in Unit B8b) to carry out a conference with each of the three children used during work on Unit B8a. Compare the results of the questionnaire with your own accounts of the children's backgrounds written in Unit B8a.

A tape recorder might be used to record the dialogue, although this does produce a lot of data for handling later. A good idea is for the teacher to listen and make notes, and for the child to see and agree with the notes which are being written. Another advantage of conducting the conference as an informal discussion is that the teacher can make further suggestions or ask questions to prompt further discussion about some point which you want to explore further.

The objective is to get the child to talk openly about his/her priorities. However, it is important to remember that the teacher is bound to exercise control and direct the discussion to some extent and that complete freedom of expression for the child is unlikely.

2   Discuss the conference with a colleague.

Did you find out more than you already knew?

Were you surprised by the items which the child found to be significant?

Were there any elements which you found that might contribute to the child's learning?

Follow-up

Were there any matters which came up that you would like to pursue further?

What problems and issues did the conference raise?

See Unit B8d for further discussion of the problems and issues in including the child's background in a profile.

Profiles and Home Background – Issues and Problems

Aim

To consider the issues and problems involved in using information about children's home backgrounds in the profile.

Introduction

If you have worked through the previous units on background information in the profile it will have occurred to you that a number of issues arise which need further discussion before we launch into a major exercise to bring in information from children's home backgrounds. There are positive things to be learned about children's achievements out of school. However, there are also some unpleasant things to be learned if we open the cupboard. Some of these are raised here; you may well think of others. It is hoped that, having undertaken the conferencing with a small number of children, you will have got a sense of whether the results of exploration of home and peer-group backgrounds is worthwhile. The points made are to help you to consider this balance. If you like, it is a health warning about engaging – or not engaging – in this kind of activity!

Method

1   As a school staff, consider to what extent you wish to include information about children's home backgrounds in the profile.

2   Consider the ways in which such material should be acquired.

Follow-up

As a staff review what you have learnt about the advantages and disadvantages of conferencing. The following comments are offered to support that discussion.

a.   How can time be organized for the teacher to carry out conferencing with children and parents/carers?

b.   Reporting the child's out-of-school achievements needs selection. Who carries out this selection? Is it the teacher alone, the child and the teacher, or should the parent/carer also be involved?

c.   Conferencing and the passing of information about home backgrounds can change the nature of the teacher–child relationship. An atmosphere in the classroom needs to be created such that the child feels able to offer information. It might be argued that this reduces the formality of relationship between child and teacher to an unacceptable level.

d.   As well as knowing about 'learning achievements' like reading, swimming and piano-playing, it can be very helpful to know of the kind of domestic activities which young children are involved in. Are they doing any cleaning up or tidying? Are they responsible for care of younger children? How far does behaviour in the classroom complement behaviour in the home? Children who tidy up at home often don't want to do it at school. Play, or refusal to play, in the home corner can give clues to this.

e.   Developing knowledge of the child's social world outside the classroom – relationships with parents/carers and other adults – can assist in the child's welfare. Once the teacher opens the way to the passing of information of this kind, instances of physical abuse as well as other stressful conditions in the child's life may well become apparent. Some authorities on child abuse emphasize the need for the school to play a part in identifying such problems. However, this does raise a number of ethical and professional issues.

How much are teachers entitled to this type of information? And how far should it be reported in a profile?

To what extent should the teacher play the role of 'social worker'?

How much professional time should be dedicated to this?

How should the teaching profession relate to other agencies: doctors, social workers?

Does knowledge of this kind of problem in children's lives add to the teacher's own emotional stress? If so, is this reasonable?

Can teachers ignore problems in children's lives?

Are we responsible for an oversight of children's lives, or just their school lives?

f.   How do we act on the knowledge which we acquire? Acquisition of more information about children's home backgrounds is likely to lead us into the need to have more contact with other professional agencies. Can this be included in the time which teachers have available? On the other hand, we sometimes spend a great deal of time on dealing with 'problem children' in the classroom. If some of these problems could be alleviated through our knowledge and intervention, then it might lead to more time and less stress in the classroom.

g.   Sharp and Green (1975) carried out an analysis of some teachers' views about the children in their classes. They found that teachers often held a 'deficit' view of working-class children, seeing them as 'less able' and disadvantaged by their home backgrounds. There is also some evidence to show that teachers tend to over-rate the support of some professional or middle-class homes and to underestimate the stress under which such children find themselves. Of course this is highly explosive territory! The question we need to ask is whether increased knowledge of children's home backgrounds will counter stereotypes, or will reinforce them. Is a little knowledge a dangerous thing here? As teachers we tend to put two and two together on the basis of what children say to us in a casual way. Would it be better for matters to be explored more explicitly and fully?

h.   What additional sources can we use to gain information about children out of the classroom?

conferencing with parents/carers (see Unit B5 on parents/carers);

information from ancillary staff about playground behaviour;

children's writing and pictures.

i.   The *RANSC Report* (DES, 1989) points to the benefits of secondary pupils recording their out-of-school achievements. However, the research evidence for the value of knowledge of out-of-school activities is mixed.

Bibliography

Sharp, R. and Green, W. A. (1975) *Education and Social Control.* London: Routledge and Kegan Paul.

DES (1989) *Records of Achievement National Steering Committee: Final Report.* London: HMSO.

Glossary

These are *working definitions,* agreed by the authors for use in this book.

Aggregation combining levels or scores of different assessments to give a single level, mark or grade.

Assessment is an ongoing process at the heart of teaching and learning. It is the way to gain insight into learning and can inform future action.

Criterion-referencing a system in which a child's achievements are judged in relation to objectives irrespective of other children's performances.

Cross-curricular drawn from and informing a range of curricular areas.

Evaluation a process by which teachers and/or children make decisions about whether their intentions were appropriate and have been met.

Evidence a variety of data (utterances, observations, outcomes—written, drawn, models, tapes, data-files, photographs) collected during learning experiences.

Formative a form of assessment that enables the positive achievements of a child to be recognized and discussed so that appropriate feedback can be given and next steps can be planned.

Ipsative a form of assessment that compares a child's achievements with her/his previous performance.

Negotiation a process that involves the child in discussion with his/her teacher (or another child) about learning goals, targets, possible outcomes and steps to be taken.

Norm-referencing a system of judging children's performance against that of others which allows rank-ordering. It can involve grading according to pre-determined proportions.

Profile an outcome of profiling that provides a 'rounded' picture of a child including a variety of elements that cover children's achievements, personal qualities and experiences.

Profiling   a process involving teacher, child and parents in assessing and recording children's achievements across a range of curricular and extra-curricular areas.

Record of achievement   a term that is used in a similar way to **profile**, but usually when it culminates in a summative document.

Recording   a method of editing, collating, summarizing and aggregating evidence of children's achievements so that they can be retained for informing purposes.

Reporting   a process of informing others about children's achievements—this could be the child, parents/carers, head, other teachers, governors, other agencies.

Reviewing   a process involving dialogue between a child and his/her teacher that focuses upon an aspect of learning to help the child identify achievements and decide on appropriate next steps.

Self-assessment   a process that encourages children to become aware of and reflect on their own achievements in a rigorous way.

Summative   a form of assessment at the end of a learning period, for recording the overall achievement of what children know, understand and can do.

Notes